BE.
THAT.
PERSON.

BE.
THAT.
PERSON.

It's not where you live,
but how much confetti you throw along the way

COLLETTE SCHOENEGGE

PALMETTO
PUBLISHING
Charleston, SC
www.PalmettoPublishing.com

Be. That. Person.

First Edition

Paperback ISBN: 978-1-68515-046-4
eBook ISBN: 978-1-68515-047-1

Cover designed by the super talented Ika Handaja

Some names have been changed.

BIG HUGE THANKS PAGE

Before I had even finished with two chapters, I realized, *I really am going to write this book. This dream is going to happen. But it can only happen if I have the time to write. Working part time will help me write this book, but it certainly won't help pay all my bills.* So, I decide to email friends and family who have been my biggest cheerleaders over the years. I tell them that I find myself at the end of my finances and want to write a book about my life and dreams. Ten people gave me money to see this dream come true. I absolutely could not have done this without those ten people. I still have some of the deposited checks on my nightstand so I can always remember that people are cheering for me.

When I got close to being finished with the book, I realized that to self-publish I will need at least $3,000. I set up a GoFundMe, and over one hundred people gave money. Now this dream really will happen. I am flabbergasted at the love and support from people all over the world. Ika, an Instagram friend I have never met, designed my cover, and it is exactly what I wanted. Megan, another Instagram friend who I have never met, formatted the final manuscript for me because I had no clue how. My friend Lori and my sister Tootie helped me with the title. It has had about ten different titles during the writing.

My immediate family is always the best thing for my soul. I can't go through one day without contacting one of my friends from Instagram. Cathy Jo, Hilary, and Tracy have listened to me talk incessantly about my book. My high school friends, my work families, my Steamboat family, and now my Cincinnati friends just add to my quiver. My Rainbow Bus friends showed me what living free looks like. My sister Tootie has been the best cheerleader and supporter along this journey. While I have loads of people to thank, my Denver/Littleton family will always hold a special place in my soul. They saw me through a dark time and rallied around me until I could become the best version of me. Palmetto Publishing was so incredibly patient with me. I had no clue how to do a Word document, but they sure do.

And to my cherished friend, my partner in life, my fellow wanderer, seeker, adventurer, kindred spirit, supporter, and my bunk bed buddy Pat: I would not be here without you. You have cheered for me and stood by me through everything, even me breaking your heart. Pat, you are that person!

This book is dedicated to Tater.

Simply the most amazing dog that ever was!

HOW I SEE THE WORLD IN THREE DEFINITIONS

Soul: The personality and identity of a person. Whatever makes them unique. That thing that sets them apart from others and is alive!

Confetti: Small strips of brightly colored paper made for throwing.

Soul confetti: Those amazing, kind deeds that a one-of-a-kind person does for another human to make their life a little lighter and a little brighter. A reason to celebrate life.

INTRODUCTION

Dreaming as a child seemed easy. Anytime anybody asked me what I was going to be when I grew up, I told them, "A physical education teacher." And darn if I didn't become one. What I didn't know, however, is that after two years I would get laid off. The principal assured me there would be a "severance package." I didn't even know what that was. As it turned out, it was money. When the check finally arrived, I decide to camp around the US on my own.

I started at my friend Jen's house in Baltimore and met up with my friend Pat a month later in San Diego. I packed a small pup tent, sleeping bag, a cooler filled with beer, books, and, most importantly, a little spiral-bound notebook, as I decided to start journaling. I felt that this trip was going to start me on a life full of adventure. As it turns out, I would end up journaling for the next thirty-five years. I didn't make it a rule like "Get up every morning and in the first fifteen minutes, start writing." I just wrote whenever.

- I wrote about my journeys.

- I wrote about things I would think about.

- I wrote about funny, ordinary things that happened in my day-to-day life.

- I wrote about things going smoothly.

- I wrote about things going horribly wrong.

- I wrote about life.

So many times, I wrote things like this:

"I desire to live a life that is exciting, dynamic, ballistic, and abundant."

"Let me be wild, different, content, and filled with joy."

"I desire more fun, more adventures, more laughter."

After 2009, when it seemed like I had lost everything, my entries started changing ever so slowly. I started writing things like this:

"I want a big soul. I want to love people, all people. It sounds easy and feels so big. I don't want to be hurtful or sarcastic or mean."

"I want to be love. I want to live a life full of zest, gusto, and adventures, all with a big heart."

So here I am, months away from being sixty years old and I wanted to see: Have I lived a life full of love and gusto? Have I become that person who hands out smiles and soul confetti to make a little difference in this world?

So I looked back on thirty-five years of journaling, and here is what I found!

CAMPGROUND RANGER

Two days into my trip, and I pull into a campground somewhere in the middle of Tennessee just as it is getting dark. There is a little kiosk at the entrance with a ranger inside. But what I really notice is a *huge* sign that says:

BE ON THE LOOKOUT!

BE CAREFUL!

DANGER!

A MURDERER IS LOOSE!

Well, that's a different welcome. I talk to the ranger and find out there was a murder a couple towns over, and the killer is still loose. Because of that, no one is staying at the campground, and if I didn't want to, he would understand. I tell him, "Well, it is either here or in my car on the side of the road as it is dark and I'm pretty tired."

He says, "Well, let's go over to this field we have. There are six huge bright lights. Why not keep all the lights on and put your tent right in the center?"

"OK," I say.

He also says he will check on me during the night. He will drive toward my tent and flash his headlights to signal that it is him. So I set up my tent. I realize I kind of have to keep my wits about me, so I decide not to have a beer and not to read my Stephen King book. It is eerily quiet—maybe it is the big bright lights? I don't even hear nighttime crickets. I lie in my sleeping bag, eyes wide open, and try to fall asleep. At some point after rolling over a dozen times, I think, *This ranger just seems too nice. Why would he do all this for me? Maybe he is the murderer!*

Sure enough, however, at some point in the night, I see headlights through the tent. I know it is supposed to make me feel safe, but it takes me by surprise and my heart starts racing. This happens again later in the night. I must have fallen asleep because I open my eyes and it seems different outside. It's natural light coming into my tent. I peek outside, and indeed it is morning. I stick my whole head out and yell, "I'm not murdered! I made it through the night!" I pump my fist, pack up my tent, and head to the kiosk. I'm beeping my horn and stop and jump out of the car to hug the ranger and thank him. I cry a little, and off I go to continue to camp across the US. For me, I wasn't murdered, so it was a great day. I didn't quite understand it at age twenty-four; I was on to the next adventure, but you see, there really are people out there who just want to help others. People who are kind and go out of their way even to help people they don't even know. I now think the world is filled with them. So, during your life, look for these people, thank them, hug them, tell them you see their kindness. Better yet, be that person.

PAT

I take my shoes and socks off. I walk to the beach, and then I sprint and jump right into the Pacific Ocean. I am screaming with excitement, and my heart is too. A month ago, I left the Chesapeake Bay, and here I am in Dana Point, California. I did it! There were days on this trip that I thought I could conquer the world, and other days I called my mom crying. Ha, but here I stand.

I am not very contemplative at this age, but I do sit down in the sand, and I know I feel different. I wonder if that guy that I saw a couple days ago at the famous Big Texan Steak Ranch in Amarillo, Texas, trying to eat that big ol' 72 oz. steak in an hour feels like I feel now. He also had a goal and a dream. As I mention, I am not very contemplative. I know this pilgrimage is the start of something different for me, but I'm unsure what. I don't think too long on the subject as I am headed to pick up my friend Pat from the L.A. bus terminal. He had spent the summer in Alaska.

I met Pat in 1985 when we were counselors at summer camps in the Pocono Mountains. He would say he was smitten with me immediately, stating, "I loved her essence, her soul, her liveliness!" I loved that he wore 100 percent cotton T-shirts and liked his chicken wings spicy. I am really amazed now looking back on how all this worked out. I had called Pat from Ohio before I left on my journey. I told him that in "about a month" I would be in California. He let me know that in "about a month" he would also be in California after spending the summer in Denali National Park in Alaska. I have my old-school Rand McNally atlas and write out the directions to the terminal.

My journal doesn't say how we ended up connecting on that day, but I think it is awesome to think about before cell phones or social media. I almost drive right by him as he hasn't shaved all summer and has a cool mountain man beard. I start honking and hollering out the window. He looks like I want to feel: content, outdoorsy, free, casual, and at peace with the world. He tells me he hasn't showered in two weeks, and I am almost jealous.

It had been six months since we have seen each other, so we catch up. He starts telling me about all these people he met up in Alaska that work seasonal jobs. They spend the winter at a ski area, head to some other tourist location to work the summer, and go back to a ski area, and so on. Yes, that is what I want. Well, we start heading east to Steamboat Springs, Colorado, as his brother Chuck has moved there now. We pull into a campground right outside of town and go searching for Chuck. When we find him, I really want to stay at his house as he has a water couch. Yes, like a waterbed, but a couch! It sits low to the ground, is kidney shaped, and a deep purple color. *O my gosh*, it was amazing!

We find out that the ski area is having interviews that weekend. We don't have any interview clothes, but it doesn't matter. We both end up getting jobs—me at the cafeteria on the ski hill, and him as a lift operator. We must drive back to Cleveland so that I can exchange my summer camping gear and clothes for winter items. I am a little nervous to tell my parents because no one has ever moved away. My dad is a teacher and just assumes I will go back to teaching. I love my family and especially my parents. We celebrate every holiday, every special event. We have fun traditions, like our annual clambake that still goes on today, and I will be missing out on all of them. I also will have to tell my dad that Pat and I will be living together. I am unsure how he might respond, and it makes me anxious.

I tell my mom and dad that I won't be going back to teaching, and instead we will be spending the winter in Colorado making $4.70 an hour, but we get a free ski pass! My mom smiles, and I swear my dad's eyes are twitching. They both do give us a hearty send-off, so I am feeling more excited now.

Off we go to start a life of seasonal work. We find this old trailer on a family's ranch to rent. Cows come up and scratch their backs on the side of the trailer, and the whole structure shakes. The wife on this ranch tans hides and hangs them outside. It is all a bit much for this city girl, but I am having a blast. The trailer ends up being so cold during the winter that we move our mattress out to the living room in front of the woodstove.

I end up meeting people at my job that I am still friends with today. One of those people is Andy. He is a huge part of so much of my life, and his name will come up constantly in my journals. He had moved to Steamboat to help his mom live out her last eight months of life. Others came from all over the US, and the group of us literally did everything together. We lived on skiing, drinking, cheap burgers, free chicken wings, and happy hour shot wheels at the Inferno Bar. As a cafeteria worker, my job consisted of me standing behind a steam table telling customers what the soup of the day was, over and over again. It was the beginning of a new way of life for me.

Look how proud I am to be making $4.70 an hour with a free ski pass.

COLLETTE SCHOENEGGE

My first Thanksgiving and Christmas without my family is hard, and when I call them, I am a bawling mess. But all these new friends are in the same boat, so we start our own traditions. Most of those traditions consist of working every holiday because we are at a ski area, but still, it is a fun tradition. At the end of the winter season, the ski area puts on this huge party for all its employees in the parking lot at the base of the ski hill. There is food, music, and kegs of beer. It is a party for the ages.

Pat heads back to Alaska for the summer, and me...well...

BURGERS, OYSTERS, AND A VW VAN

If you ask my sister Marilyn, she will give you a different account of our trip from Cleveland to Massachusetts. She was dropping me off on Cape Cod so that I could catch a ferry headed to Nantucket Island, where I would be working for the summer.

My journal entry from 1987 says this:

Marilyn and I are having such a blast. We have the windows rolled down, singing at the top of our lungs, and laughing a lot. We stop, and I get Pepsi and gummy bears. At night, we end up at this sketchy hotel. But I am so psyched to be working on Nantucket for the summer that it doesn't bother me. She drops me off two hours early before the ferry is supposed to depart. I cry and tell her I love her. I am waving like a fool as she drives away. Here I wait. I have my backpack, my trusty sleeping bag, and my bike.

Her rendition is this:

Collette played the same Jimmy Buffett cassette tape on repeat for ten hours. Sometimes, she would rewind a song and sing it over and over again. I ask her if she brought any other cassette tape, and she tells me, "Yes, twenty-five of the world's best polka songs." We stick with Jimmy Buffett. She had all the windows rolled down, and it was like forty degrees outside. Every time we stop, she picks up a huge 32 oz. Pepsi, which makes us stop more for her to go to the bathroom, and she picks up another Pepsi, and, well, you get the idea. We end up at a hotel that charges by the hour (wink, wink), and it has no sheets on the bed and no lights in the hallway. I drop her off early at the ferry so that I could get home. I throw the cassette tape out somewhere in Massachusetts. *P.S. We really did have fun, though, and laughed a lot, and you should have seen her waving goodbye and running after the car yelling, "I love you, Marilyn!"*

I arrive to work at this super fun, fast-paced restaurant as a line and prep cook. The restaurant, called The Brotherhood, is known for hand-patted burgers, spiral-cut french fries, and amazing clam chowder. When I say we are popular and super busy, it isn't just me overexaggerating, as I am known to do. On the days that I prep, we hand-pat three hundred burgers. Today, if you would put ten pounds of ground beef in front of me, I could pick up 5 oz. on the first try. It is also a place that, as an employee, you can charge food and drinks to your paychecks. Paydays were always kind of a "do over" for me. A rebirth in budgeting, if you will. I would declare, "OK, no more shift beers for me!"

It is an amazing, fun summer. I sail, play tennis, hang at the ocean, work (a lot), and fish from the beach—surf casting. (OK, I don't really ever catch on to this. You are supposed to run toward the waves with this huge fishing pole, and when you reach the water, you cast the line out and hope to catch Nantucket bluefish. I broke one pole and tangled a bucket full of fishing lines.)

I end up picking up a second job because of that "charge to your paycheck" thing. I help out on an oyster farm. Yes, you ride out in a boat to a small, shallow inlet in the ocean, jump in the water, and use these little rakes to scoop up oysters from under the sand. If they are big enough, you toss them into a basket that has been tied around your waist. Sometimes we open oysters right there and eat them. (Sometimes, there may or may not be vodka for oyster shots.)

I laugh, though, because of all these amazing things I did on this stunning 6x15-mile island, when people ask me about my time there, I always talk about the night a guy from work asked a bunch of us to just tool around with him in his old VW van. He called it his "road canoe." All we did was drive 35 mph all over the island. I have never felt more myself. That van ride gave me a dream that has stuck with me. I long to have my own road canoe. Yellow, of course! You really never know where your dreams will show up. For me, it was a gorgeous island thirty-one miles off the coast of Cape Cod. Be ready!

MY WORK FAMILY

The end of the summer brings Pat and me back to Steamboat Springs. I cashier at the cafeteria this year. Same friends, same hilarious times, same funny antics, same traditions of working every holiday, and same type of living arrangement. This time it is a cold apartment underneath the entrance to an apartment complex, which allows us to hear everyone walk in and stomp their feet. There are no windows, so if there was a fire, the only way out is the front door. After my friend Jen from Baltimore came out, she remembered having layers and layers of clothes on, shivering from the cold—*but* we had free ski passes.

My friend Jen and me sometime in the 1980's

BE. THAT. PERSON.

I realize I could write another book on my years spent in a Colorado ski town in the late 1980s, and maybe I will. I loved every job I worked, which included a concierge, a waitress, a flower gardener, and I even worked an outdoor BBQ in the middle of the ski hill, all with these new friends who are like family. While I had hundreds of memories, my most amazing memory is a vanload of us traveling over two and a half hours from Steamboat Springs to Red Rocks Amphitheatre to see Jimmy Buffet. We had taken all the seats out of the back of our van, and we sat there with a battery-powered blender making margaritas the whole way down and singing Jimmy Buffet at the top of our lungs.

When life stopped for me in 2009 and I lost about everything I knew, including most of my friends, these companions, these friends, called and supported me. Kenny, if you are reading this, I saved your voice message for years. If I ever felt down in the dumps, I would listen to that message and laugh, and my spunk would return. You gave me a bit of your soul confetti when I most needed it.

I have found that the folks I end up working with at my jobs are my extended family. It's just who I am.

MY MANAGER CATHY

The summer of 1988, Pat drops me off at my friend Jen's house in Baltimore, and he takes off to drive back up to Alaska. I will spend the summer working on a fishing boat, so I call the owner the next morning to tell him I have arrived and can start anytime. The phone conversation goes something like this:

ME: "Hi, I am here in Baltimore and can start work."

HIM: "You're a female?"

ME: "Yes, yes, yes, I am."

HIM: "We don't hire women."

ME: "I filled out the application and got a call that said I got the job."

HIM: "The person must have thought Collette was a guy's name."

ME: "But I talked to him on the phone. Well, why don't I come on the boat for a day and see if I can do the work and then decide?"

HIM: "We don't hire females!"

ME: "OK."

Well, I sit there and wonder what the heck I am going to do all summer. I can't just live here at Jen's house and not work, and do I want to stay in Baltimore? The next morning, I wake up and say, "Why not call Pat and drive to Alaska with him?" I try and remember who he said he was staying with in

Minnesota the next couple days. Ugh, why don't I ever remember people's names, or at least pay more attention when people talk to me?

It takes a while, but I do remember the person's name. Yay!

This is before cell phones, so I have to call 411, Information, to get his number. Reading this now seems funny what with cell phones, but 411 was the thing back then. They connect me, and, sure enough, Pat comes to the phone, and he is indeed headed for Alaska the next day. I ask him to pick me up at the Minneapolis airport, and I will go to Alaska with him for the summer. None of this seems off the wall to either one of us. He fetches me, and we head to the local REI outdoor store as I don't have my sleeping bag with me. And off we go to the last frontier.

I find out that you don't just drive to Alaska. You need a copy of the travel guide *The Milepost*, which we have. It is a very detailed guide for travel on the Alaska Highway, called the Alcan. Even if you never drive to Alaska, the book is fantastic. It is a very thorough book on camping, fishing, gas stops, restaurants, and services that also gives history and even has a planning guide. When I Googled to see if it is still around, I saw it is! It says it weighs seven pounds!

We are using it mostly to see where the next gas station will be, but I read fun facts now and then to Pat. When we cross from the Yukon into Alaska, a customs worker tells us, "Please be very careful tonight if you are stopping. There is a suspicious man running around and is dangerous."

I, of course, think, *Two years later and that murderer from Tennessee made it to Alaska.* We drive away, and when we finally stop for the night, it is too dark to put up our tent. There is not enough room in our truck to stretch out, so we sleep under the truck for warmth and for safety. Again, this doesn't seem off the wall for us. Guess what?

I wasn't murdered again! I have a good track record.

We arrive in Alaska, and I don't have a job, but I do have a new purple sleeping bag.

What I do find before a job, though, is a fun women's softball team to play on, the local coal mine, Usibelli Coal Mine, was the sponsor. I have played on many teams in many states, but this team is by far the most talented team I have been a part of. Some of the players wear hiking boots instead of cleats, and it doesn't seem to matter.

Because the towns are so far away from each other, we end up traveling to tournaments every weekend. Anchorage, Fairbanks, Wasilla, and Palmer are some of the towns I get to see, all because I play on this softball team. The first tournament we are headed to, the gals tell me the first game is at eleven.

"Oh, good" I say. "I play best in the morning."

They look at each other. "11:00 p.m.!"

"Oh, yay. I have always wanted to play under lights."

They all just stare at me—literally stare and just start laughing. "It won't be under the lights; it is still light outside!"

Hahaha, yes, of course!

Sure enough, we play many games that start at 11:00 p.m. or even midnight. We end up having some amazing weekends together, sleeping in tents and winning lots of tournaments.

I get to see the northern lights while sleeping outside in the middle of Denali National Park.

I get to climb a mountain on June 21st to watch as the sun never sets. It hits the horizon and bounces right back up. I have a picture somewhere of me wearing sunglasses at 1:00 a.m.

I get to take a ferry from Alaska to Seattle where you sleep outside on lounge chairs. It is unbelievable, traveling down the Inside Passage, waking up and seeing dolphins or whales just playing in the water.

I take a helicopter tour all around Mount McKinley.

Bears, oh my, tromping all over Denali National Park.

Once, I try getting my mail but can't get into the post office because of a herd of moose at the entrance.

I eat salmon and halibut that have just been caught.

My brother gets married this summer, so I fly back to Ohio for the wedding. I mention this because flying in and out of Alaska is pretty cool. Just when you think that you are going to fly straight into a mountain, you land and start heading toward water. And just when you think you are going to end up in the water, the plane stops and you realize you have been holding your breath and squeezing the hand of the person next to you. You also get to fly in and out of so many cities. $900 may sound expensive, but I got to see the airports in Anchorage, Seattle, Denver, Detroit, and Cleveland.

And...

I do find a job! I get to work right at the entrance to Denali National Park at the employee restaurant. We cook breakfast and lunch for all the staff. My boss, Cathy, teaches me to cook and bake and has so much patience with me. We make soups, fish, breads, and desserts. She introduces me to the Moosewood Cookbook. I fall in love with cooking, and guess what? It is still one of my biggest passions. Was it because my manager took the time and shared her love and I fed off her zeal? I don't know, but I do know that cooking will be a huge part of my future years, all because someone sprinkled their confetti into my life. Think about your passions and how they came about.

Garrett Oliver, the brew master for Brooklyn Brewery, says this: "That one thing you think you can do better than everyone else—go out and do that. The light shining out of your eyes should blind people."

MORE SOFTBALL AND GOLF

Pat has some brothers getting married in the summer of 1989, so going back to Alaska wouldn't be the best financial decision. We end up in northern Michigan with our friends Bill and Laurie from Steamboat. We end up living with them in this cool farmhouse in Beulah. I find a job at Crystal Lake Golf Course helping in the little café or sometimes taking the beverage cart out and selling drinks to the golfers. The best part of this job: the owners, the other staff, free golf, and Labatt's beer on tap. It was such a wonderful golf course, and I will end up going back a couple summers to work here again. I play golf almost every day, and the owner even gives me a few lessons.

Of course, I have to find a softball team to play on. The funniest part of this team is our sponsor, Bill's construction company, called Bullseye Construction. Our shirts have an enormous target on the front, and our pitcher always feels a little uneasy.

Because I am finally geographically closer to my family, my parents actually get to come up and visit. Yay!

COOKING CONTEST

My mom would say the only reason I went into the kitchen growing up was to get to the backyard. I had no desire to cook and just wanted to hang out with my friends and play sports. At some point in college, I perfected French toast and crepes and made those two things incessantly one whole summer while on break.

Soooooo...it is funny that, for thirty-five years, most of my jobs were in the food industry and that cooking is a huge passion.

In 1990, President George Bush declares a couple times in the media that he doesn't like broccoli. The Campbell Soup Company and *Woman's Day* magazine pick up on this and collaborate to do a "How to Get George Bush to Eat Broccoli" recipe contest. The only rule, it seems, is that you have to use Campbell's cream of broccoli soup. I decide to enter the contest. I alter my friend Andy's recipe by stuffing it with broccoli and ricotta and tossing the soup on top. I send the recipe off, and life goes on. I really never think about it again.

Months go by, and now it is 1991. One day, there is a knock on the door, and a certified letter is handed to me. My mind immediately goes to a couple weeks back when my friend Kenny and I had gotten kicked out of a bar for something involving me yelling from the dance the dance floor, *"Play Jimmy*

Buffet!" I yelled this over and over and over again. The band got tired of me yelling, and apparently so did the bar. *But...*

It isn't that! This is a real telegram, like one from *The Sound of Music* real!

It tells me that I won first place in the "How to Get George Bush to Eat Broccoli" contest.

What?

I run to try and find the magazine that has the contest in it to see what the prize is, but I can't find it. I do find the phone number and decide to call *Woman's Day* to make sure. They say, "Indeed, you won in the dinner category." They go on about the recipe and how they decided to slice the chicken breasts when they were cooked because they think it is a better presentation and is that OK with me. No problem with that, ma'am! I finally tell them I can't remember what first place was, and the woman responds, "$2,500."

I am flabbergasted! "You are going to send me $2,500?"

"Yes, it will be a couple months, and your recipe will also be on label of the can of cream of broccoli soup in certain areas of the country."

I hang up and call everyone I know—yes, everyone!

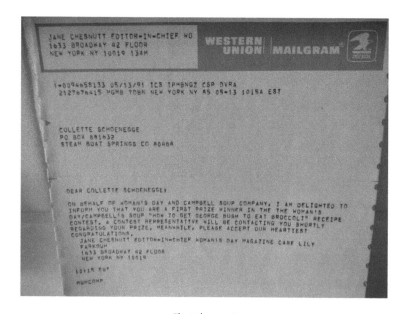

The telegram!

Also, I have at least ten *Woman's Day* magazines with this winning recipe in it!

First Prize: Meat, Poultry, Seafood

COLLETTE SCHOENEGGE'S CHICKEN-BROCCOLI CANNELLONI

- 4 boneless, skinless chicken breast halves (about 5 oz. each)

- ½ cup ricotta cheese

- 3 T grated Parmesan cheese

- 1 T chopped onion

- Pinch of pepper and Italian seasoning

- 4 large fresh broccoli florets with about one inch of stem, cooked crisp tender, drained, cooled, and cut in half lengthwise

- 1 can (10 ¾ oz.) condensed cream of broccoli soup

- ¼ cup water

- 4 oz. shredded mozzarella cheese

- Parsley for garnish

Heat oven to 375 degrees. Pound chicken breasts between sheets of plastic wrap with a meat mallet until ¼ inch thick. Mix ricotta and parmesan cheeses, onion, and seasonings. Spoon across center of breast halves. Top each with two pieces of broccoli. Roll chicken up from narrow end around filling and broccoli. Place seam side down in a nine-inch square baking dish. Mix soup and water. Pour over chicken rolls. Sprinkle with mozzarella. Bake uncovered for 35–40 minutes until chicken is opaque near stuffing when tested with a knife. At this point, you can serve how you like, or cut into thin slices like they suggested.

BASEBALL

Is it because I grew up going to see the Cleveland Indians and the memories of those games are such a part of my essence?

Is it because I love the sounds of the game? The person selling concessions up and down the aisle, yelling, "Cold beer!" The crowd singing "Take Me Out to the Ball Game." The ump yelling, "Play ball!" The crack of the bat when the ball is headed straight at me during batting practice.

Is it the pace? Slow, then fast, then slow again.

Is it the smells? The green grass, the hot dogs, the sun.

Or is it that as an adult, I can wear a baseball mitt and big foam hand for three hours and no one seems to care?

I guess it is all those reasons. Baseball is a *huge* passion of mine. Even with some things that other fans may not like: players constantly changing teams, player strikes, interleague play, the designated hitter, the use of Jumbotrons, ketchup and mustard races (I do especially like this), *I love it all*! I have been to games for the rookie league all the way up to the major leagues with a couple independent league games thrown in. It is my dream to see a game in all thirty major league ballparks in one summer, traveling to each stadium in my yellow VW van.

How do I even pick my favorite games over the last thirty-five years?

1. My dad, Pat, and I head to a Thursday day game; they used to call them "businessman specials." We come so close to seeing a no-hitter. It goes into the ninth inning. There are only ten thousand fans in the stadium. We are all standing and cheering with such gusto my throat hurts for days. But the visiting team gets a hit, and we were two outs away from seeing my first no-hitter. It is simply awesome!

2. Pat and I head back to Ohio in the middle of summer in our old red Chevy pickup truck to go see my family. We realize the Kansas City Royals are playing a day game, and we will be driving right by the stadium. It's a no-brainer. However, we are still dressed like we live in the mountains of Colorado, so we change into shorts and tank tops right in the open cargo bed in the back of the truck. It is muggy, steamy, and downright sweltering, but we get tickets three rows back from first base. The stadium at this time is still Astroturf, and you can feel the heat coming from the field from where we are sitting. It is like sitting in front of an open pizza oven. The clouds come quickly, and so does rain. All the fans start running for cover, and Pat and I sit there in our seats with rain pouring down and me yelling, "Yay, this feels so good!" Steam is coming right off the field from the rain hitting that baking Astroturf. We sit there laughing with how great it all feels.

3. 2003—Pat and I go to a three-game series of the Cleveland Indians vs. the Texas Rangers in Texas with dear friends of ours from Fort Worth. Rafael Palmeiro for the Texas Rangers is one homerun away from hitting his five hundredth. Friday night, he doesn't do it. Saturday night, all four of us head back again to see if we will see history. Cleveland is winning in the top of the ninth, and it doesn't look like Raffy is going to be back up to bat, so we decide to leave. When we get to the car, we turn the radio on, and Rafael is up to bat! *What?*

I declare very loudly, "Ugh, I knew we should have stayed!"

I can still hear the announcer today exclaim, "It's a long fly ball! Could this be his five hundredth?"

I am yelling, "No, no, go foul!"

"Foul, by inches," the announcer says.

We sit there in the car for minutes just laughing. We head back to the park on Sunday afternoon, and he does indeed hit his five hundredth homerun. The ushers come around with certificates to prove we were at the game.

I also get to sing "Take Me out to the Ballgame" with Harry Caray at Wrigley Field in Chicago.

I am at a game in Milwaukee County Stadium to watch Bernie Brewer with his foam head descend a long slide right into a big vat of beer after a player hits a homerun. (This happens to be a dream job for me!)

The best baseball memory, though, didn't even involve being at a game.

MARRIAGE, BASEBALL, AND JOE CARTER

Early in the year, Pat and I start talking about maybe getting married. I tell him that would make my dad so happy. This was Colorado in the '90s, and the state considers us legally married because we have the same checking account. I get my health insurance and my free ski pass through him as he is now on full time/year-round as a lift electrician, so the ski resort considers us married as well. But we both decide to go ahead and do it. September 6, 1991 would be the date, back in Macedonia, Ohio (suburb of Cleveland), where I grew up. It's funny, though, because I just never thought I would ever get married. I didn't have a dress picked out in my mind when I was younger. I never practiced walking down an aisle with someone holding up my wedding dress train. I didn't date people and wonder what our kids would look like, and I never practiced writing my name with someone else's last name. It just seems right. I know without a doubt that Pat will love me and allow me to be me.

I will spend a couple months back at the golf course in Michigan so that I can drive down during the summer and find a place for the wedding and a wedding dress. I find a fun restaurant with a great outdoor patio, and the mayor of Macedonia said he could perform the wedding. I go dress shopping with my mom and sister and end up finding the perfect knee-length dress within an hour at Sears of all places. I put it on, we all look in the mirror, and we all start crying, so we know it is the one. It takes me most of one whole day to find a slip for under the dress, and don't ask my sister Marilyn about that, because she went with me and declared at the end of the day that she would never go shopping with me again, and she hasn't! I ask Andy to be my maid of honor because he is my best friend, but he refuses, saying, "You will make me wear a dress I will never wear again."

All seems to be working out. About a month before the wedding, I am still in Michigan, and Pat calls one night to inform me that he has "given his life to Jesus Christ." I had no idea what that even meant or how it would affect me. He seems the same, but I get nervous. I call Andy and ask him to get together with Pat and report back his findings. I need to know if Pat has gone off the deep end or if I should just go ahead with the marriage. Pat always has had a huge heart and a big soul, thinking of others, and always peaceful. The joke is that I am the storm at the center of his calm.

Andy calls back and reports that indeed Pat is still very much himself. He is doing great, but he seems to talk about Jesus a lot. Well, I still don't know what to do. I buy a six-pack of beer and sit on the beach of Lake Michigan all night. I decide in the wee hours of the morning that if this is something weird or strange, Pat will be smart enough to get out of it, and if it is something awesome, Then it will all work out OK. I go ahead with the wedding plans. Pat comes to pick me up the week of the wedding, and we take off for Macedonia, Ohio. What has happened though, is my dad has decided to run for mayor of Macedonia. Suddenly, the mayor is "busy that day and can't perform the ceremony." The wedding is Friday, and it is Tuesday. We need to find someone to officiate the wedding. (Once again, writing this sounds so unrealistic as in most states now, anyone can perform a wedding, including the two getting married.) But this is 1991 in Ohio and is not the case. It is now Wednesday, and friends from Steamboat, Michigan, Alaska, and most of Pat's relatives are starting to show up. My dad has called pastors all over the city, and we still can't find anyone.

"Too short of notice."

"If they do a three-day marriage retreat, then yes."

"They were living together, so no."

Well, now it is Thursday. In twenty-four hours, we should be getting married. Everyone attending the wedding is now in town. I start wondering if indeed we will be getting married, if maybe this is some magical sign. Pat also has doubts, and we both wonder if we should just call the whole thing off. My mom and sisters and I decide to go out to eat and get our minds off the whole situation and see what happens. There sit my dad and Pat in my parents' living room. Pat announces, "I'm going in the backyard to pray!"

So, there he stands right next to the dog fenced area and he prays, "God, I love Collette and would love to marry her. However, I now love you, too, and want what you want in my life. If I am supposed to marry her, please let me know."

My dad, retelling the story for years later, says this: "Pat announced that he was going to the backyard and pray, and what was I to say? That really is all we have left right now. Pat tells me that God will tell him if he should marry Collette. Again, I didn't argue with him. Three minutes later, the phone rings. It is a minister friend of mine who heard we were in a bind and needing some help with Collette getting married. If they both can come meet with me for an hour today, I will officiate the wedding."

My dad yells to Pat, *"Your prayers have been answered. We have a minister! My friend Reverend Jennings."*

Reverend Jennings has a big soul, and we would go see him whenever we were back that way. Another person came into my life and sprinkled his confetti all over my soul.

All of us girls came back, and Pat and my dad tell the story so fast and loud that we are laughing and cheering and hollering. OK, if you know my dad or Pat, you are correct that Pat isn't telling the story so fast and loud. He can't get a word in.

Because of winning the cooking contest and our love for baseball, we will be taking whoever wants to go to the Cleveland Indians vs. Toronto Blue Jays game that night for our rehearsal dinner. It ends up being about twenty people. This is 1991, and the Indians aren't having a great season. Cleveland Municipal Stadium seats about seventy thousand fans. We walk right up to the ticket window and ask for twenty seats together. This time, I run into the stadium with friends and family, and the smells and sounds seem a little sweeter. That night we had our names on the big Jumbotron, and the rest of the night was spent listening to Andy yell, "Hey, batter, hey, batter, batter, swing, batter"—for three hours straight.

Here we are celebrating our wedding at the Cleveland Indians game the night before our wedding.

Friday is a perfect fall day, seventy-five degrees and one cloud floating in the sky. My mom, dad, and I walk onto the patio to Kathy Mattea's "Battle Hymn of Love."

My dad speaks to start. We all cry.

A bee flies up my mom's dress. We all laugh.

Pat and I say, "I do." We all cheer.

The keg is tapped. We all drink.

The DJ plays music. We all dance.

But this isn't all—now here is the biggest surprise of all. One of my favorite baseball players at that time is Joe Carter. He had played for the Cleveland Indians, but then he got traded and now plays for the Toronto Blue Jays, who are in town, as you know. When he was in Cleveland, he had a small ownership of the restaurant we got married at. I had no clue about any of this. The owner of the restaurant was a friend of my dad's, and they set it up to have Joe Carter stop by. Yes, a famous ball player gave up free time to come to a crazy baseball lady's wedding. I can't stop hugging him and patting him on the back. He finally has to tell me he has a sore back. Ha! Yep, he has a big soul! It is epic.

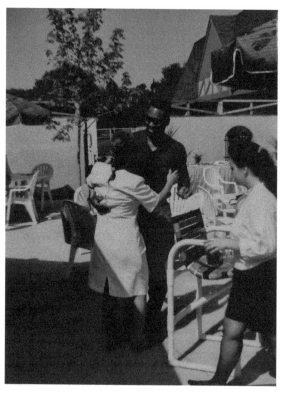

Yay for Joe Carter!

BE. THAT. PERSON.

Our plans get changed a little because of shenanigans that happen that night after the reception involving my old high school track, beer, and a chain-link fence, so we have to drive Pat's brother's truck back to New York as his brother has a sprained ankle. I follow behind in our van with a "Just Married" sign on the back, and it is rather funny because Pat's teenage cousin is in the front seat next to me. Whenever people beep and wave, I yell out the window, "This isn't my husband!" So funny. We spend three weeks doing what we do best, traveling around the US—New York, Vermont, Poconos, North Carolina, Texas, Steamboat.

Life seems to be going along smoothly once we get back to Steamboat. Pat is on full time as a lift electrician, and I concierge in the winter and take care of all the flowers at a resort and golf course in the summer. I work a couple nights a week at the Chart House restaurant. We have an awesome trailer right on the Yampa River and fall asleep to the sound of the river flowing every night, and we love our friends. I was very content, indeed.

ME, A PASTOR'S WIFE

Pat comes home from work one day, in 1994, and says, "God spoke to me today in the lift shack."

I say, "Are you sure it wasn't one of your coworkers on the radio playing around with you?"

"Nope, it was God. He told me I need to become a pastor."

I have always had a small problem of speaking before I think; this time is no different, and I blurt out the first thing that comes to my mind.

"Pat, you have a stammer and a stutter, and I am not sure public speaking would be the best thing for that."

I am also realizing that I don't live near a beach, so I can't just grab a six-pack of beer and sit on the beach all night and decide if he has gone off the deep end. I can't just stand here with my mouth and eyes wide open, so I actually speak from my heart.

"Pat, as you know, just recently I started my own spiritual journey with God, and this whole idea of being a pastor is kind of scary for me, but I will support whatever dream you have. If God told you this, who am I to argue? Go be a pastor; I will be right there cheering you on!"

Later in the night, I realize that will make me a "pastor's wife." I get a little alarmed and wonder what that even is.

BE. THAT. PERSON.

Things move rather quickly, and, in the fall of 1994, we move two hours and two thousand feet higher in elevation to the Winter Park ski area and the town of Fraser for Pat to start seminary and start the pilgrimage of becoming a full-time pastor for Fraser Valley Baptist Church. I will start my own pilgrimage with God. I packed my skis, my mountain bike, ,my bible, and my gusto. I felt ready.

My journal entry after my first Bible study at this new church goes like this:

Pat is teaching a Bible study, and I am there with about ten other people. He is talking on and on and keeps referencing scripture. I say as quietly as I know how, "Where the hell is that?" I cover my mouth quickly, and the person sitting next to me doesn't miss a beat and points it out to me. I feel like this is going to be a good fit.

PRAYER AND RUNNING

Reading back on all these years of being a pastor's wife, one thing is true: I prayed! I have fifteen notebooks filled with nothing but prayer requests. If I knew you from 1994–2009 and you even mentioned that your aunt's best friend had bunions, she was prayed for. If you were wondering how you were going to pay rent, I prayed for you. Nothing was too small or too big. I prayed. Pat and I had one heck of an epic fifteen years and would say that this blossomed our friendship but also challenged us. There were things that happened during this time that really shaped who I am today and added to my dreams.

Some of the awesome, unforgettable things:

- a mission trip to Honduras to build a health clinic

- working the 2002 Winter Olympics in Utah

- heading down south to help with cleanup after Hurricane Katrina

- going to Maui so that Pat could perform a wedding on a private beach

- friends and I going to see Brad Paisley perform at Greeley Stampede (a huge Colorado western festival), and a seventeen-year-old singer by the name of Taylor Swift opened for him.

- starting a women's spring retreat in Moab, Utah

- working loads of fun jobs at the ski area and in town—serving as ski school phone reservationist, managing a kitchen at a retreat center, and waitressing at a fun, busy restaurant—and three years of not working and concentrating on just being a pastor's wife, working at the church's funky, awesome thrift store

- being the Bible teacher at many women's retreats, the highlight being a weeklong canoe trip down the Colorado river with Bible students

- started a laundromat ministry where people could come and do their laundry for free

But when I look back on all these years, what really stands out is that I was meeting with, mentoring, encouraging, rooting for—whatever word you want to use—women of all ages. It is my passion to cheer for other women to inspire them to be themselves and to become the best version of themselves because they really are beautiful, and the world needs them. I still like telling women to stand out, shine, be colorful, and "be uniquely you."

I met with many in those fifteen years, but two of these awesome souls stand out because they handed me a passion that is still with me and continues to be a part of my life. Their names are Tammy and Connie.

In 2003, I was meeting with Tammy and Connie every Saturday morning. The three of us are reading Richard Foster's book called *Celebration of Discipline*. We would read a chapter every week and get together and talk about each chapter. When we finally finish the book, I ask very pastor-wife-type questions: "Well, what will you take away from this book? How has it changed you? What do you want to do or not do in response to reading it?"

I think for sure they will answer something about prayer, fasting, fellowship, or, at the very least, chastity. What Tammy says is "I want to run a marathon!"

Connie replies, "Me too!"

I am bewildered, astounded. Again, not thinking before I speak, I say, "That just doesn't sound very spiritual, and on top of that, I can't run twenty-six miles!"

It's like they don't hear me and continue with their excitement. "It will be all kinds of discipline."

I am still very skeptical. Tammy says she has been reading this book called *The Non-Runners Marathon Trainer*, and this book is what gives her the motivation to do a marathon. She tells me to take her copy of the book and read it on my vacation that I will be leaving for next week. If I decide after reading it that I don't want to run, then the three of us could come up with something else. I take the book with me to Ft. Worth and end up reading it through twice. I am hooked! Had I had a cell phone, I would have texted immediately. Instead, when I get home, I call Tammy and say, "*Woohoo!* Let's do this!" We decide on a fall marathon in Boulder, Colorado, called "The Boulder Backroads Marathon."

We start training. Being a new runner, I just assume that any shoe will do, and I find an old pair of Nike shoes in the lost and found at the church. A week into training, and I get shin splints. I call a friend who is a runner, and they say, "Oh, you just need new shoes. Go down to the Boulder Running Company in Littleton, about an hour and a half away from Fraser, and they will get you on a treadmill and find the perfect shoe for you."

Pat and I head there the next day. When I walk into BRC Littleton, I feel like I am home. Everything about the store feels like a big hug. An employee meets me as I walk in and says, "Hi, my name's Donna. What brings you in today?"

We become instant friends. She doesn't judge me for having old shoes; she doesn't laugh when I tell her I am not a runner. I tell her about training and living in the mountains. We end up talking about everything. She gets me in a pair of shoes with an insert and a new pair of shorts. When we leave the store, I turn to Pat and say, "I want to work here some day!" I would think of reasons to go there as it made my soul smile.

BE. THAT. PERSON.

We follow the training plan from the book, and I *fall in love with running.* It is all I talk about for sixteen weeks. I talk about my runs, my new hat, my new shorts. Anyone who walks by me gets a story about my fourteen-mile run or my love of Gatorade. Call anyone and they will tell you! We live in Fraser, Colorado at nine thousand feet, surrounded by six hundred miles of single-track dirt trails, and I feel alive!

September 28, 2003 is absolutely beautiful without a cloud in the sky. A bagpiper plays at the start line, and my journal from that day is pages long, detailing every mile, every person I met and ran with, Pat and all my other friends who came out to cheer and high-five me. The moment I cross the finish line, I am crying and say, "I can't wait to train for my next one."

I go soak my body in Boulder Reservoir with a cold beer and a smile on my face that just won't go away. Two huge passions come out of this experience that stay with me today: running and helping women go through life by cheering for them.

At the finish line of my very first marathon.

GENE

I board the Amtrak train in Granby, Colorado, to go see my family in Cleveland, Ohio. I absolutely love the train. It is so different than flying. You hand your luggage to a coach attendant, and they put it in this huge closet where you can get to it anytime. The train I am on is a double-decker, and I walk up to find a seat.

I don't need a sleeper car because the seats are so huge, and they have footrests and recline back. If you are super lucky, you get two seats next to each other all to yourself and can really stretch out. On this trip, I am really lucky. When we arrive in Denver, I am excited to go into Union Station to see the inside. Once inside, an announcement comes on: "Please be aware of your surroundings and your belongings. There are pickpockets around." I thought pickpockets were only a part of the play *Oliver!* so I head back to my train.

I meet so many people. You can walk to all the other cars, but the best is the observation car where the seats all face out and the walls are all windows. I had brought my own food, but I head down to the snack bar to grab a couple small bottles of wine. I grab my cheese and crackers and go to the observation car to watch little towns pass by and talk to everyone who sits or passes through. It gets late, so I head back to my seat. No one has taken my pillow, blankets, or anything. People on the train are trustworthy.

At one stop in the night, two police officers come on to the train and take the two guys sitting behind me off the train. Apparently, they were smoking in the restroom, and this is a nonsmoking train. You don't want to cross these Amtrak rules! When I wake up the next morning, we have just left Omaha. They announce that Ottumwa, Iowa, will be a smoking stop, so people can get out and smoke or just walk around. I decide to go out and look for a Sunday newspaper and a Pepsi. I find the Pepsi but no newspaper. When I come back to the train, I see it pulling away. I start yelling, *"Stop, stop, stop that train!"*

A man working the train station comes out when he hears me yelling.

I say, "Allmystuffisonthattraineverything." I was talking so fast. "My suitcase is in that big closet! My books, my food, my backpack, my wallet, my ticket, my pillow, my blankets!"

He states rather calmly, "There is no way to stop the train."

I stand there crying, as if that would somehow bring the train back. He takes me inside so I can use the phone. I call my parents and bawl some more. They assure me all is OK, and they can wait one more day to see me. I try calling Pat but must leave a message. I have a little bit of money on me as Pat told me to carry some cash, just in case. Here is that case!

I find out the man working the station's name is Gene. He tells me there is a motel called the Stardust just outside of town, and he can drop me off there. He also asks if I would like to stop on the way out there to see Roseanne Barr's house. I decline the side trip. He asks what seat I was in.

I say, "I don't know the number, but I can describe exactly where is was and all the people around me."

Gene tells me he will radio my train and will get all my belongings off at the next stop and have them put all my stuff on the next westbound train. He will go meet this westbound train and retrieve all my belongings when it comes through that night and bring it out to me at the hotel. I am still in shock that he is doing all this for me. We drive to the hotel, but the front desk isn't open, so a housekeeper lets me inside an empty room. Sure enough, around 9:00 p.m. Gene knocks on the door and has all my belongings—*everything.* Train people really are trustworthy. I finally get in touch with Pat and tell him the whole ordeal. He says, "You are in a room, watching baseball, eating stuffed crust pizza. It's really a perfect night for you. What is the matter then?"

I say, "I didn't have closure."

"What?"

"Yes, I met all these fun people. We were like best friends. I was going to get their addresses and become pen pals. I didn't get to say goodbye or anything. I was just gone."

Later in life and even now, I realize I still don't like *not* having closure. It's the reason I don't go to yoga classes. You see, it's a super quiet class and you must be calm. You end up in a fetal position and breathing calmly, and the instructor says, "OK, when you are ready, get up and leave the room quietly. Namaste."

What? I want us all to get up together and see if anyone would like to go out for breakfast burritos.

Gene and his wife and kids actually come back in the morning to pick me up and take me back to the train station. I am an hour and half early and refuse to leave the station. Gene is another one of those people who touched my life with his big soul. Who runs around Ottumwa all night just to get some woman's belongings to her? Who then loads his family in the car to come pick me up and drop me back off? I will tell you who! A person with a big soul. A person who makes a difference in this world by touching others with his soul confetti. I really do start thinking the world is filled with these people.

When I board the train in Ottumwa, I walk around and tell everyone my story, and they all seem to agree that it was unusual. I have a layover in Chicago. The train station is bigger than some airports I have been in. My journal says I got a chocolate shake, so it must have been good for me to mention it. I ask over and over if I am on the right train. People must have thought I had memory problems until I tell them my story. Everyone ended up knowing my story and would yell funny things: "Hey, don't get off at this next stop! Is this the right train?" We all got a laugh out of it. At 2:30 in the morning, the attendant comes and wakes me up to say we are almost to Cleveland. When I get off in Cleveland, there is my dad waiting for me. We hug so hard and then hug some more. When we get home, my mom is awake, and we stay up and talk for an hour.

No matter what city I am living in or visiting, I know the Amtrak train whistle. Every time I hear it, it brings a huge smile to my face. And I say a huge thank you to Gene for being that person!

MY DAD

The summer before my sophomore year in high school, my dad asks me if I would like to go out for frozen custard. Of course I do. While we are eating our cones, my dad says, "Collette, you have been dating Jim for a couple months now, but he will be leaving for college next week to go play football. I just wanted to let you know that when he gets to college, he most likely will not call you anymore."

"What do you mean, Dad? He told me he loved me."

"I just want you to be prepared is all."

Guess what, everyone? Jim left for college and never contacted me again. How did my dad know? I think some dads just know.

My dad would sit in the stands during my track meets with a stopwatch in his hand. When I would come up to see him after my races, he would ask my time and see how close he got. He came to all my track meets, and if my college rugby games were close, he would come to those as well. He taught at the high school I attended, and I couldn't wait to have him as my teacher. I never did because he said I would talk the whole time and he would have to send me to the principal's office. Usually, it's the student who doesn't want their parent for a teacher—ha! Not me.

When I was in college and when I moved out to Colorado, he wrote me a letter every week. Yes, every week. He would add a funny comic from the newspaper and sometimes a couple bucks.

He directed plays for the high school, community theater, summer theater, and any other theater you could think of. When I think of him, I think of someone gregarious and someone who had a commanding presence. He was the best storyteller. You just wanted to sit and listen.

We would drink Genesee Cream Ale in 16 oz. bottles and call them Genny Pounders or Foster's beer in those big oil cans. When Coors beer finally came to Ohio, we were the first in line at the store to get it.

He bought the first microwave oven when they came out. He couldn't wait to cook a beef roast in it. It said twenty minutes, but he didn't believe it, so he put it in for an hour. It was beef jerky and the size of a dollar bill. We ordered pizza instead that night.

I loved him. Plain and simple. I would make it a priority to go back to Ohio at least once a year.

September 1998—I board a plane in Denver to go see my family in Cleveland. The lights dim in the airplane, so I can't see Pat inside, but I know he is praying and waving to me. I am trying to wave back and tell him that I forgot to write that check he asked me to write. It's funny to read back on how afraid I was of flying, because now if I board an airplane, I am taking pictures out the window, talking to everyone, drinking a beer, and trying to get a book out of my backpack.

But in 1998, I was afraid of flying. I would write things like:

- "How is the flight attendant just standing there talking like nothing is wrong?"

- "How can this person next to me be sleeping?"

- "I can't hear what they are saying about the length of the flight or the weather."

My parents are both inside to pick me up. (I miss people being able to come inside and greet each other.)

I have the best two weeks with my family. The Cleveland Indians are in the playoffs, my dad takes me to see the new post office, we go to West Side Market, and we play a *ton* of cards. Our family card game is called Back Alley Bridge. It is different from the Hoyle card game with the same name. Our game is created by and for my family. It is the highlight of every trip I take back to visit. We talk, yell, scream, laugh, shuffle, deal, bid, and have a blast.

We have played Back Alley Bridge for decades, so as you can imagine, we have loads of memories. The game that gets talked about more than any other game went something like this:

It is the last hand of the game; we all get dealt one card. Clubs are trump. If my brother takes the trick, he wins, if my dad takes the trick he wins. My brother turns his card over and stands up to declare victory as he has the king of clubs. My dad starts screaming and we assume he is mad about losing. He then also turns over the king of clubs!!!! We had played the whole game with duplicate cards! My grandmother declares Paul the winner as he played his card first. I will spare you the family fight that followed. I am happy to report that we now laugh about this today.

Pat arrives the last five days and gets to enjoy all the fun. Our flights back are great. We get back into Denver and then drive to Fraser and get home by midnight. We have a beer and head to bed.

We get up early as Pat has to work, and we see there is a message on our answering machine. (I miss those old machines!) It is my mom. My dad had a massive stroke early in the morning, and he is in ICU unable to speak or move his left side. We drive back down to Denver, and in the last twenty-one hours, I have been in and out of three different time zones. This time when I board the plane, my palms aren't sweating, and my heart isn't racing. I am just crying, looking out the window. When I see my dad, I cry some more. This charismatic, dynamic man is now just staring blankly ahead. There will be no more letters from my dad, I realize.

The two weeks I am here are filled with days that all run together. To the hospital by noon, stay nine hours, back to the house, sleep, and then back to the hospital. We take turns going to therapy with my dad. Therapy is pretty limited and involves him trying to pick out a yellow paperclip in a box of blue ones. He doesn't even understand that. I am spent but also thankful that I didn't have anything to resolve with him. While we may not have agreed on everything, there was never a point where I didn't love him. The nurses let us know that we are looking at long term care for him as he should have been improving by now. He will never come home. I decide to head back to Colorado and see what happens next.

My biggest memory of my dad, of course, is a baseball game. In 1995 on the famous "Get off in Ottumwa" trip, I talk my dad into going to the new Jacobs Field in Cleveland. He said he wasn't ever going to another game during the players' strike the year before, but he does say he can't wait to see the new stadium. So, May 7th, we head to the park for a day game. We get there before the gates open, and they blow this loud factory whistle to announce the gates opening. Walking into a ballpark is still one of my favorite things to do, and this day is no different. I run in and go look at the field first and stand there smelling the smells and smiling wide. We have to walk all the way around to our seats, so I grab us both beers for our walk. We get seats right in the sun, and it's a "beautiful day for baseball!" Hot dogs with the famous stadium mustard are a must! My mom says she will put dinner in the oven about three hours after we leave, and we can eat when we get home.

Well, it was tied at the end of the ninth inning. It goes to the tenth, the eleventh, the twelfth, the thirteenth, the fourteenth. We finally decide we better head home and, let's face it, they stopped serving beer in the seventh inning! We listen to the game on the radio on the drive home. It ends up going seventeen innings and is still the longest time game in Cleveland history. Cleveland won. When we get home, my dad and I tell my mom about the stadium and the game all while eating cold pork chops. My dad's face got so burned from sitting in the sun all day that for a week we could just peel sheets of skin off it. I think of this game every time I think of my dad. I am so glad he agreed to go!

My dad was a great whistler, taught me how to drive a stick shift, and had a strange way of telling when the spaghetti noodles were done. He said that if you throw a noodle on the wall and it sticks, it is done. I know whoever bought our house found noodles randomly on the kitchen walls and probably thought we had had a food fight.

Three weeks after I had headed back to Colorado, there is a huge windstorm one night, and Pat suggests we open all the windows and let the wind come through our apartment while we sleep. I have never known Pat not to sleep with a box fan on, but tonight he says he would like to listen to the wind. At 3:15 a.m., I hear the phone ring. Had we had the box fan on, I never would have heard it. It is my mom.

That night, November 18, 1998, my dad died.

Death and grief are as hard to describe as they are to go through. It is a raw feeling in my soul that lingers for months.

World's Best Dad!

TATER!

January 26, 2008, a three-to-four-year-old basset hound named Tater jumped out of her foster mom's car and right into my life. She had spent the last years as a breeder mom in a puppy mill and needed a forever home. From that moment, my life was filled with more!

More adventures, more love, more excitement, more journeys, more joy, more kindness, more zest, more antics, more passion, more thrills, more miles, more smiles. Tater showed me how to live life. We were inseparable. Her answer to anything I asked of her was yes! She and I would end up being soul mates.

Tater and me, July 2008

I DON'T LIKE THICK SKIN

I start noticing something different in me sometime in 2007. I can't quite explain what it is, but I just keep telling Pat I want to do something different. I would say being a pastor's wife was challenging and hard, but everyone has a difficult thing in their life. Some people would say teaching is hard, others that parenting is hard, and others that just getting out of bed is hard, so it wasn't that. There were plenty of amazing times, it was very rewarding, and Pat and I really did put everything we had into the church, but I felt that I was starting to get thick skin. I don't like thick skin on me. When people would complain or say unkind things, I wouldn't even let it hit my heart or soul and would declare to myself that their words meant nothing, but really, their words didn't just bounce off me—they stayed on my skin and made it thick.

One night, two couples have us over for dinner, and just as dinner is wrapping up, one of the men says, "You know why Robert died, right?" Robert was one of the founding members of the church, a great human and someone who loved all people. He had gone to the hospital for a very routine procedure and ended up dying on the operating table. The man continues, "Pat and Collette, Robert died because you two weren't at the hospital. Had you both been there, he wouldn't have died!"

BE. THAT. PERSON.

My heart starts racing, my eyes squinting. I try opening my mouth, and nothing comes out. About five minutes later, I still haven't even spoken, and I make eye contact with Pat to tell him that we have to go.

As soon as we get in the car, I am almost screaming, "Pat, people cannot treat us like this. I will not put up with it any longer."

Pat suggests we take a couple days off to decompress. *Sigh*. Not the answer I was looking for.

So, we took time off, and I went right back to growing thick skin.

WILD AND FREE

I don't have to read my journal to see that 2009 started out difficult but ended up being that point in my life when I made hard decisions that cost me just about everything.

A fun, epic weekend in early January is just what I need but isn't what my knee needed. I do an amazing two-hour run through snowy trails on Friday. Saturday is a five-hour snowshoe adventure, and on Sunday, I am on the ski hill snowboarding all day. By Sunday night, I can't walk. I take ten days off all activity, and my knee still isn't any better.

I head to an orthopedic surgeon who specializes in sports injuries and sit through an MRI. I hope to get the results back in two to three days. The next day Pat and I fly into LaGuardia as his uncle had died. Funerals are both soothing and heart-wrenching to me. We spend time with Pat's family, which is special, and the celebration of his uncle's life is sad and joyful all rolled together. The weekend is topped off by taking the Jersey transit into New York City for the day—Central Park, the Theater District, Wall Street, an Irish pub to watch some of the Super Bowl, and then, just as the sun is setting, we go up the Empire State Building. It is absolutely magical. Before we head back to Colorado, I call my doctor and set up surgery a week later for my torn meniscus.

The surgery goes awesomely. I am on the couch that night with Tater right next to me. Because I wanted to start running sooner rather than later, the doctor suggests I don't use crutches and start physical therapy in five days. I get up from the couch and walk down our driveway, limping but so happy. Tater is so cute and actually limps with me. Someone stops and asks if Tater had gotten hurt because they noticed her limping.

I start physical therapy at a place known for getting people back out and active, and the physical therapist ends up being a trail runner just like me. Her name is Abby. This is where my heart starts noticing something different. She must be the only person in this small town who has no idea that I am a pastor's wife. In fact, she just assumes I am a lesbian just like her. Each session, I ask more and more about her life and start thinking, *This is what I want, to live with my dog and run trails.*

When I can finally start running, she joins me, and with her help, I end up running a half marathon four months post-op. While that should be the end of our time together as I am done with physical therapy, she mentions this six-day bicycle event called Ride the Rockies. Each day, you ride your bike up and down mountain passes with anywhere from thirty to eighty miles per day and elevation gains over the six days of about twenty-five thousand feet. She and three other friends are doing it, but each person needs to have a support vehicle (SAG vehicle). She asks if I would like to come along and be her support vehicle. It would be seven days of driving her car to the next camping spot, hauling her equipment and gear, and cooking dinner at night. *Absolutely!* I can't not go. I need it.

I can't take Tater, and Pat says they will have a fun week together.

That they are all lesbians isn't even a thought in my head. I just love being around them. They are easy to like. They have a great friendship and a whole lot of fun living life.

The SAG vehicles have lots of time before we must get to the next stop, so we play tennis and take pictures all along the way. I am making new friends. One of the friends, Paula, just makes me feel so alive, so free, so unhindered. She and I play tennis and pickleball in the grass, and we cook and laugh. I had heard of Paula, as she has some important job at the ski area and her partner, Liz, is an Olympic skier, but they are so much more than this. They are this awesome family that accepts me right away. I refer to them all as my Rainbow Bus friends, and I want to get on this bus and be free. Paula and Liz would end up helping me for years after this event.

One morning, the bikers take off, and I say that I am going to go on a trail run as we are camping right next to the Gunnison River. It is already superhot out, and at the end of the run, I am sticky and steamy. I deviate from the trail a little bit and walk down to the Gunnison River. I strip all my clothes off and jump right into the flowing river. I swim up to get my head above the water and let out a big, huge "*Wahoo!*"

This, this is what I want! This freedom, this contentment, this happiness is what I desire. I am so full of life as I lie on my back looking up at a beautiful sky and amazing canyon walls. I think we all have a picture in our mind of when we loved who we were. This is mine.

I get home, and I am content, colorful, and confused. I get together with my Rainbow Bus friends to camp and then finally see the slideshow of the bike event. I call Paula to see if we can get together. We drive around, and I tell her that I may or may not be in love with Abby. I go on to explain that it is so hard because Pat is such an amazing man, and the ripples of this decision will be wide.

She says, "Collette, no matter what you decide, we are here for you. I am so glad we are friends!"

August 16, 2009

One friend from the Rainbow Bus lets me use her condo, I don't have a mattress or a bed, but it is a great place to decompress. Here I sit in Fraser, Colorado, and am now separated from Pat. Tater isn't allowed in the condo, so she and Pat are at our house. I really haven't moved much, and I reach for my journals. I find it odd that I have been journaling for decades, and there is no mention of the heart ablation I just had a week ago. This is how lost and confused I am right now. Camping around the US on my own now feels like a walk in the park. My journey to becoming the best version of me is about to start.

LITTLETON, HERE WE COME

After meeting with the church counselors and Pat, it is suggested that I move to Denver. This will help the church heal and move forward and hopefully help me to sparkle again. I agree as I do think being away will allow me to get the alone time I need. When I get back to the condo I am staying at, I write this: "All I need is a job, a place to live, and money." That's all!

I decide to look for a place to live in Littleton, as I want to apply at... Boulder Running Company. I call and set up a time to come talk to the store manager. The interview goes great, but he says they aren't hiring right now. He isn't sure when they will be, maybe another month or so. I am crushed. I did not see that coming. In my mind, I get the job, and Tater and I start our life in the charming small suburb of Littleton and live happily ever after. So now, I must start looking for a job. I think, *Well, I am alone, confused, scared, unemployed, and broke* but *hopeful!* I don't know if it was how I grew up or a personality trait, but I always just think things will end up working out.

I still have a flip phone at this time, and Pat and I are sharing a laptop. When I do get the laptop, I get on line and quickly apply for 20 jobs. Not one of them gets back to me. I am headed back down to Littleton to look at two places to live, so I decide to stop along the way down to apply for jobs. I stop at pizza parlors, bagel shops, fine dining restaurants, golf courses. I don't stop at any coffee shops because I don't like the smell of the coffee shops. I love coffee, just not the smell that stays on my clothes when I leave.

I fill out so many applications that my fingers feel stuck. I am a forty-eight-year-old woman who can't get a minimum wage job. I now am starting to realize why people stay with one company for thirty years; they just don't want to interview or fill out applications. I am tired, and maybe I am starting to lose that hope I had.

I do have two places to look at to rent. I need three things: a place that takes dogs, has lots of sunlight, and has a bathtub. The first place has all three. It is super cute, and I can imagine how my bed will look up against one of the big windows with Tater's bed right next to mine. When I talk to the rental person, they ask, "What kind of dog?"

"A basset hound named Tater. Here is a picture of her."

"Oh, shoot, we don't take basset hounds."

"What? Oh no! "

But they do agree that Tater sure looks cute.

The next place I look at is right on Main Street in downtown Littleton. Main Street is super charming with cute shops, restaurants, bars, galleries, old buildings, and is dog friendly. Linda, the building manager, meets me at the door of the apartment building, and we take the elevator up to the third floor and walk into an end unit. I love the place! It has lots of natural light and big windows. It is newly painted, and the walk-in closet is bigger than the bedroom. I can even imagine where Tater and I will put our Christmas tree. They take basset hounds! I fill out all the forms, and she needs a deposit and first month's rent. I tell her to hold it for me and I will see if I can get the money. I call Paula and Liz and tell them that my and Pat's house has a contract on it and a closing date, and I ask if it would be possible to borrow money so I could get this cute apartment.

"Absolutely! We will drop a check by later."

These two have big souls!

Would you like to know how my mind works? Well, I had just three things I needed for a place, and this cute place has all three. Now I wish it had a gas stove instead of electric and a nice balcony. Ha ha, but I am one for three. I have a place to live. I also pick up a local paper and find a restaurant close to my new apartment that is hiring for a line cook. I set up an appointment for that Friday.

Friday comes, and I feel hopeful about this job interview. When I walk in, it seems crowded, which is a good sign. I meet with the general manager, and we get along so well that they have me then meet with the head chef. I get a tour around the kitchen and get introduced to other cooks who are working. All seems great.

He says, "We would like to have you start Tuesday."

"I would love to start Tuesday!"

"OK. It's getting busy here now, so I will call you on Sunday night to tell you what to bring for your first day."

"Perfect!"

If I didn't think it would embarrass me, I would have done cartwheels the whole way out the door. I can't wait to tell Tater the great news. I get to the parking lot and realize I don't have my car keys. My heart starts racing, and I almost feel panicky. I have lived twenty plus years in a small ski town, and I have a super old car, so I never lock my doors. Most times, I just leave my key in the ignition. I know exactly where my keys are. I walk over to the car, and, sure enough, my doors are locked and there are my keys with all my fun key chains hanging from the ignition. I start crying. Life is like that, really. One minute, I am doing cartwheels because I have a job. The next, my keys are locked in my car. I decide to go back into the restaurant to see if they have a hanger or something else. That is all I need for my old car. There is now a line to get in, and I make eye contact with the general manager.

She comes over. "What's up?"

"I locked my keys in the car and need a hanger or something."

"What?"

"I locked my—"

"I don't have time for this. I can't just leave the host stand to go find you something to unlock your car."

"OK."

I head back to my car, and my phone is also in there. I can't call anyone either. Maybe I could use the restaurant phone. Ha ha, who would I call anyway? Tater? But I see a construction site right up the road. I walk over and see a man about my age.

"Hi. I locked my keys in my car. Do you have a hanger or something?"

"Heck yes, I do. These kids that work for me do it all the time. Hang on."

OK, so here it is, late Friday. I am sure all he wants to do is pack up and head home and start his weekend. But, no, he comes and opens my car. I, of course, hug him and tell him when I get money, I will stop down and give him some. I also let him know I will be working at the restaurant right there. He goes there all the time, he says, and will see me soon. Big soul!

Isn't that how life goes? A yay, an ugh, a yay! I head back to the mountains and tell Tater all about our new place and my new job. I promise her she will have fun. Sunday night comes, and I never hear from the head chef. Monday comes and still no word. I finally decide late Monday to give him a call as I needed to know what time tomorrow. The chef lets me know that they decided to hire someone else. I don't even feel that hope that has kept me going. I am crushed. Was it because I locked my keys in the car? I will never know. I sit in this condo I have been staying at and I stare. I know what I should be doing:

- reminding myself of all the things I do have

- telling myself it will all work out

- calling my family as they would cheer me up

- looking for jobs

But I can't do any of that. I can only sit on this couch and cry. That seems easy to me. Crying feels so good, but it gets me so tired. I am wiped out but cry most of the night. I wake up and go on a run and realize I can't cry all day; I need to find a job. The phone rings, and it is a Denver number. I am so thankful that maybe some place is calling me back.

"Hi, this is Collette."

"Hi, Collette, this is Dennis from Boulder Running Company. We can hire you!"

"Yes, yes yes!" My mind is telling me not to tell him the whole story, but my mouth doesn't listen. "I just found out I didnt get this job at this restaurant and I cried all night!"

"Ummm, when can you start?"

"I can be there in about an hour and a half."

"How about Thursday?"

Even though it was suggested that Pat and I only talk about our house selling or Tater, I call him anyway. "Can you believe that in 2003 I declared I would work there someday, and here I am."

Hope and crying got me through.

FREDERICKE

I call a great friend of mine who has been in touch and has been such a huge cheerleader for me at this time. Her name is Fredericke. She and her family have basset hounds, and they are Tater's best friends. I tell her I got the job at BRC and that on September 1st, I can move down to my new little apartment right on Main Street. For this next week, I will just commute the hour and a half each day.

"Oh, Collette," she says, "I have a week at a hotel to use that I will just let you have. I will find one right by your workplace."

I start crying because, once again, a big soul filled with confetti shows up in my life. The hotel will be a mile from my work. I sleep in a real bed for the first time in two weeks.

LITTLETON, OUR NEW HOME

Tater and I are back together and sitting in our new little apartment. I have a lawn chair, her bed, my trusty sleeping bag, and some kitchen items. I forget bath towels, so I use kitchen towels for a couple days. There is a friend from church who says she can use the church van to help me move the rest of my belongings down. The only day she can do it though is September 6th—yes, Pat's and my anniversary. I really don't know what to do. I am only moving some shelves, pots and pans, and the kitchen table, but I say OK as I am more thrilled that she reached out to me. Abby agrees to help as well.

In the end, it is a miserable decision. I can't do anything but stand in the kitchen of our house and cry. I forget most things and just want the day to end. I end up bringing an ironing board but no iron—when was the last time I even ironed anything? Tater and I drive together to our new home, our new life. I have my Jimmy Buffet cassette tape playing in the car, and Tater doesn't seem to mind like my sister did. The church van chugs behind.

$125 OF AWESOMENESS

I do something next that makes no sense to anyone but my mom and me. You see, a long time ago, someone told her, "Sometimes you just have to do something for your soul." I am moved into my place, Tater has food, and I have about $130 on a credit card. As I mentioned, the apartment is right on tree-lined Main Street. I walk out of my apartment, and I can walk right into a pizza place or one of the many funky shops. There is one store that has all these hip and sassy clothes. It is such a modern shop, and the window display is filled with all these colorful clothes and a clawfoot bathtub filled with balloons and trendsetting items.

I walk all around, and my eyes and soul are drawn to this pair of jeans hanging there. I run over and wonder about the size. They are a European size, so I take them off the hanger to go try them on. When I get them on, my heart starts fluttering. It has been so long since I have had a new pair of jeans, and these feel incredible and look wonderful. I keep turning around in the dressing room so that I can see them in all different angles in the mirror. I absolutely have to have them. I felt downright free-spirited.

I speak aloud and say, "Jeans, you are coming home with me!"

I take them to the register and tell the cashier over and over how they made me feel. She gets such a kick out of me. She puts them in a fancy bag with handles. She says, "That will be $125.34."

My eyes pop out! Now my beating and excited heart stops. I never thought to look at the price as they are just perfect. I hand her my credit card and wonder if the sale will go through. It does, and I realize that is the last of my money.

That was 2009, and I continue to wear those jeans. They now have patches and a smiley face on them. Even now when I put them on, I feel free spirited and all *me*! The picture on the back cover is me in those jeans. Sometimes you really do have to just do something for your soul.

EMAILS, EMAILS, EMAILS

I just assumed that the tough part of this new way of life for me would be

- leaving Pat,

- finding a job,

- finding a place to live,

- moving to a big city,

- and figuring out if I was in love with Abby.

As it turns out, the difficult part is the emotional part. I still have a flip phone, so when Pat is around Denver, he drops off the laptop. I open email after email that start with or include:

"In my quiet time today, God told me to tell you..."

"While I was praying today, God gave me scriptures that he wanted me to share with you about sin in your life."

"Just thought I would send these scriptures on what God thinks of homosexuality and divorce."

"I am praying that your and Pat's marriage get restored. But it won't happen without you praying."

"Collette, you aren't praying enough."

"The only thing God wants is for your marriage to be restored."

"You realize you have ruined a church, a valley, and a marriage."

"If you had fallen in love with another man like I did, it would be different."

A handful even tell me that I am no longer welcome in the valley and please don't ever come back. Every day, about twenty to fifty emails. Over and over again...

I don't care how strong a person I am or how much I depend on God during this time, each email makes what little spark I have get dimmer and dimmer. You see, this isn't about me just moving down to Denver to sow my wild oats or go through some midlife crisis. This is a turning point for me in my life. I can either become magical or lose myself in what other people think. While I was writing this book, I asked Pat to write me a paragraph on what he was thinking when I left. Here is what he sent me:

"At the time, and unbeknownst to me, you grasped a reality better than your current situation and made the very brave choice to eject yourself. To exit the safety and comfort of the known, security, and sustenance for a liberated life. That is one of the bravest, dynamic, life-changing moves I have witnessed. I continue to be extremely proud of you for going against conventional wisdom and societal norms! You are a brave and happy soul. And I love who you be!"

I mention all these emails to a friend, and they suggest changing my email address and my phone number. But I don't want to do that. I shouldn't have to do that. They will continue to stop by at my work like they are doing now. I figure I will be old news soon; something else will happen, and people will move on.

While not in the same magnitude, these emails continue for over a year. I don't have the capacity at this point to love all people and to forgive, *but* I want to, and that is the difference right now. I want to make something so beautiful out of this mess. I may not be ready emotionally or mentally to love right now, but I do try to answer a few of the emails with what I am feeling, what I am going through. For me, I was losing my dreams and my passions and losing myself, and I wanted them to support me in finding my way and my voice again.

My replies are mostly this:

"Please pray that I get restored, not so much my marriage."

"I don't need to be fixed; I just need a friend."

"This isn't about being a lesbian or a pastor's wife. This is about being Collette, being fully me!"

"I am reading a book right now about God waiting forty years for the Israelites to stop wandering. I believe he can wait on me."

I don't reply to the very heated emails.

A person stops in at Boulder Running Company. My heart is pounding when I see them come through the door. *Why come here?* I wonder. I meet them at the front of the store.

They say, "Hi, Collette. I hear you moved down here with your girlfriend."

"Nope, no, I didn't, just Tater."

"Oh good, because that would make me sick to my stomach."

I head to the bathroom and cry. Another person wants to get together for coffee. I am hesitant, but again, I am trying to keep thinking the best of people. And I am hoping she wants to apologize for the email. I tell her there is a Barnes and Noble right next to BRC—let's meet there.

When I sit down, she says, "I really just wanted to see what lesbians wore to work."

Like I said, I want to love, and someday my soul will be alive again and the light coming out of my heart will be seen for miles. Today doesn't seem to be that day. I ask a person from the church for a small loan to help see me through the next couple of months. They tell me to go without eating as they won't give me any money.

Amid all this, though, is my amazing new job. Every single time I walk in the store, I still feel like someone is hugging me. I am making friends with my coworkers, and they are absolutely the best. Donna is still working there, and our friendship grows. Another gal is Sara, who has such a loving soul, and we meet for coffee, tea, or sometimes donuts. She gives me cards and poems to help me along this journey. Then there is Steve, who becomes my kindred spirit, my pal, my companion.

They all become like family to me.

I do think they think I have some kind of stomach or bowel issue as I spend so much time crying in the employee bathroom. But they just keep loving me. I want to learn how to love, how to forgive, and how to be different than other people. I want a *big soul*! It is so hard to wade through my circumstances, but it is my quest to come out of this more beautiful and more compassionate. To become magnanimous!

NELLIE

The first friend I make down in Littleton is Nellie. She also just started to work at BRC. That she is twenty-five years younger than me doesn't matter. That she is this superfast runner and I like to plod along and take pictures—again— doesn't matter. What I love is her gentle, soft spirit. I like that she seems to cry easily too. Her heart is so compassionate. I figure she must have gone through something in her life to make her soul shine. One day she tells me about be- ing inside Columbine High School during the horrid shooting. It is so hard to listen to, and at the time, we are unaware that in a couple of years she will go through yet another tragedy.

She jumps right in to help with BRC women's run group, Saturday run, and the BRC race team. We work all the time together. When her first child is born, I hurry to the hospital to see her, the baby, and her husband. That little boy is only a couple hours old, and I get to hold him.

While writing this book, I read an entry in my journal that said this: "I sent a text to Nellie apologizing. I haven't heard back from her yet, and it has been a whole day." I didn't mention what I needed to apologize for. I can only surmise that I spoke without thinking or said something that was hurtful. Be we remain friends today, so our friendship even made it through that rocky time. Just a side note then—apologize if you need to. Friends are worth it.

While I mostly remember her helping me with every single Saturday Run and how awesome she was at fitting people with a pair of running shoes, I won't ever forget my first Christmas in Littleton.

It is sometime after Thanksgiving, and I have a heart-to-heart talk with Tater.

"Tater, I know last year we had the best time ever cutting our Christmas tree down, hiking all through the snow to find the perfect one, singing Christmas carols, and eating festive cookies, and I told you this is now our tradition. But this year, I just don't have the money. We have to go without a tree."

She looks at me, and I do believe she says, "You have to believe, Collette."

"Yes, Tater, indeed, we have to believe. Let's just keep repeating that over and over. We have to believe; we have to believe."

Well, one night, Tater and I are starting to get ready for bed. It is 8:00 p.m., after all. There is a knock on our front door. I just assume it is a neighbor as someone must buzz you into the building, so I go over and look out the peephole. I can't believe it. There is a friend of mine from the church. I get a little nervous as I hadn't heard from her in ages.

She says, "Hi, Collette, what do you need?" as if I was the one knocking.

My heart is racing, and I know I look confused. "What do I need?"

"Yes, like really, not like a better prayer life or spiritually or emotionally. What do you need in life right now?"

Tater is standing there next to me, and I can feel her push her nose on my leg. "Oh yes, we need a Christmas tree!"

"A Christmas tree?"

"Yes, a real tree, not fake, never fake." I tell her the whole story of how Tater and I would believe it would happen.

"Well, let's go get one."

"It's eight o'clock."

"Yes, we can go to Lowe's. Tater can even come!"

Off we go in her truck. We find the perfect tree, and she buys us a tree stand too. We sing Christmas carols and bring that tree right up the elevator. Wow! I don't have any lights or decorations, but I had believed, and, sure enough, Tater and I had a tree.

A couple days later, I am at work and Nellie comes in. She is off that day. She walks over to me and says, "Collette, my mom and I were just at Target, and I didn't know if you need any Christmas ornaments, but I bought you a couple boxes because they reminded me of you." They all had polka dots on them. I stood there crying, of course! I told her the whole story, and now I had ornaments too. Every Christmas I bring those ornaments out, and they remind me of my friend who has a big soul and shared it with me.

Nellie!

WOMEN'S RUN GROUP

I walk back to see our store manager, and I say, "I am absolutely loving this job, but what I miss most about Winter Park is all the women I would run with. Do you think we could start a women's run group?"

"Sure! Let's set up a meeting so you all can decide on what day would work. I will send out an email right now."

"Wow, just like that? I have three more presentation points I didn't get to."

So, Nellie and I start a run group. One will be an early morning run from the store, and another will be a night trail run. The first morning one is at 6:00 a.m. on a Tuesday. I end up running with a gal named Susan. She has such a calm personality and I seem to be drawn to people like that lately. I end up telling her my whole ordeal: pastor's wife, Littleton, Abby, Tater, Pat...She just listens and asks good questions. Later at work, I think, *Holy cow, that woman will never show up at another run. I can't believe I told her everything. It did feel good, though.*

She did indeed show up again, and again, and again. We remain close friends today. So, really, if something feels right about a certain situation and you feel a tug at your heart, follow it. It may just bring about a close friendship.

This running group somehow turns into a Thursday night and Sunday morning trail running group that ends up becoming my best friends, my family, my tribe, my people! We do everything together.

The highlight each July is celebrating Kim's birthday at Lakeside Amusement Park. One year, they all get together and get me a laptop for my birthday. Yes, a laptop. I am typing on it right now. I spend Thanksgiving with some of them and even go to Myrtle Beach. We see each other through all life events. Every week, we run together, and the bond grows deeper. I do believe if I called any of these friends today at three in the morning, they would answer! (Maybe I will try that!)

CITY GIRL

Tater and I seem to be in a groove. I mean, I am still a hot mess, still trying to learn a new job, get used to apartment living, find new trails for Tater and me to run, and find my spunk, but I am learning things about living in a big city. I had to find a dog park for Tater as they have leash laws here and dogs can't just run around and be free-spirited. Tater never leaves my side at the dog park, so I decide just to run with her on all the trails with her off the leash. I get written warnings all the time.

I stop in the grocery store to drop off my thyroid prescription. I walk around a little bit and then head back over to pick it up. The conversation goes something like this:

"Oh, hi. Did you need another prescription refilled?"

"No, I am just coming back to pick mine up."

"Didn't you just drop it off fifteen minutes ago?"

"Yes, that was me."

"It will be ready in twenty-four hours."

"Hmmmm, OK."

But still the best of me learning about city living is this:

After months working at the store, I realize that I may need to get a second job. Thoughts of filling out more applications and interviews, however, are not what my mind needs right now, but my checking account does. During my drives around Littleton, there is a place that always seems to have openings posted outside on a sign. One day, a front desk person, another day, a janitor, another day, mail room help needed. I decide to go in and see what they may have open.

"Hi, I would like to apply for a job."

"Which one?"

"That is what has me a little worried, you see. I think it may be a red flag that you are always needing workers. Why do so many people quit here?"

Blank stare, no answer. Thirty seconds, and still a blank stare, no answer. I wonder if perhaps I have something in my nose.

Finally, she speaks—very slowly—"We. Are. A. Temp. Agency."

"Hahahahahahahaha, of course, that explains it."

I am still just shaking my head thinking about her telling all her friends this exchange tonight over drinks. She gives me the name of a seasonal outdoor ice rink that will be hiring for the winter, and off I go. I get the job and end up working with all high school boys who talk about hockey, girls, and taking their dad's Viagra before they go on dates.

CITY LIFE AGAIN

Besides running buddies in the mountains, I also miss grilling out. I go down to Linda and ask, "Would it be possible for me to bring my gas grill here, set it up in the parking lot when I use it, and then store it under the stairs in the parking garage?"

"We can only do charcoal grills here, and I would have no problem with you storing the grill under the stairs. Hi, Tater—love your bowtie!"

I go out and buy this little portable charcoal grill that sits about six inches off the ground. Tater and I sit there that night grilling brats and drinking beer in the parking lot like we don't have a care in the world and that there aren't pickup trucks and yellow parking lines everywhere.

I love routines and newspapers, and I seem to have both right now. The newspaper delivery person even brings the Denver Post up the three flights of stairs and leaves it right at my door. I have just come back from having a root canal, and even that seems to be OK. Pat and I closed on our house in Fraser, and after paying Paula and Liz back, I buy a sofa and an area rug. Tater and I sit on that sofa all night and keep saying it feels like sitting on clouds.

But I also realize I really am tired emotionally, physically, and spiritually. After I get off work, I take another late-night walk with Tater, and we find this grassy area next to an office building. The grass is so soft and spongy, so we just lie down right there. We both realize how much we have missed grass, and this grass feels phenomenal. The next thing I hear is "Look at that awesome hound dog." I shake my head, sit up, and say, "Oh, oh, yes, thanks." We had fallen asleep on the grass. When we get home, I look at the time. We had slept there for over an hour.

BE. THAT. PERSON.

I remember being so confused when I moved to Littleton, and my journal certainly suggests that as well. So, reading back is hard now because I am reading it through different eyes, if you will. I am in a better place now, but I did feel these things and it is my story. It is what made me who I am today.

I was reading a book at the time called *Chasing Frances*. It is a fiction book about a pastor who finds himself broken with no faith. He heads to Italy to gain new life and new perspective. He gets introduced to how St. Frances of Assisi lived his life, and he finds healing. In the book is a quote I modified for myself: "In the end, God isn't going to ask you, 'Why were you not Moses?' No, he is going to ask you, 'Why were you not Collette?'" The quote sees me through this turmoil. I am spending too much time on the wrong questions. I want an end point. But the question is so much bigger than my feelings for Pat or Abby.

Who is Collette?

I can't just take off to Italy to bring me up out of the water again, screaming "wahoo" like I did in Gunnison, Colorado, so to help me wade through this time, I decide to see a counselor. Someone who doesn't know me or anything about the small mountain town I had been living in. The first visit, she cries more than me. The second visit, I tell her all about Tater. She says

73

we treat our dogs the way we want to be treated. On the third visit, we start dealing with my emotions. We talk about hurt and forgiveness. She suggests I write letters to people, not with the intention of sending these letters, but for the purpose of allowing my true feelings to come out. She assures me it will be good for my soul. I end up writing twenty letters that week. I do feel my soul start to come alive a little. For the longest time, I didn't want anyone to read what I had written as the words seem so raw and personal. She said I would never send these, but now I find myself ready to share three of these letters because it was a big step in becoming my full self:

My Letter to one church family.

Pat and I moved over here from Steamboat fifteen years ago, as you know. You were there when Pat preached to the church to see if they wanted to call him to pastor. You voted yes. You came up to me after the service and said, "Oh, Collette, you have a different last name than Pat. You kept your maiden name. We don't do that. We will never use your last name, and it will always be Pat and Collette O'Connell."

At that time, I thought, "Of all the loopy things I have done in my life and that is what you have a problem with? Well, I am OK with that." But I really should have said something then, because from that point on, I always felt so deficient around you. I do think that you and your wife tried to support us, but how it was done was very hurtful to me. You would offer your opinions of the church yet never asked how we were doing. You just told and suggested things that we could be doing better. Again, I realize now I should have talked to you and explained how I was feeling.

I now realize that it is OK to tell people how they are impacting me. It can be done with love and not to hurt or blame. While feelings are not always true, they are real. It really came to a head in 2007. I understand that you were very hurt over the death of Robert. He was one of the founding members of the church. He and his family have supported and encouraged Pat and I since we first moved over here. He was a steady, peaceful man, not only in the church, but also in the community, and I do know he was a very good friend of yours. It was an absolute shock to hear that he died on the operating table during a pretty basic procedure. Pat and I spent days crying and meeting with his family. However, for you to tell us that Robert died because Pat and I weren't at the hospital is not only far-fetched and unlikely, but I also feel it was almost abusive. I couldn't speak that night after you said that. I got home that night and told Pat that you could no longer treat me or us like that anymore. I now need to set some boundaries with you. Pat and I did the absolute best we could for the church. We are called to love, but there is also truth in that love. I know you are hurting right now, but I believe that Robert would have died whether Pat and I were at the hospital or not.

My letter to Abby

Abby, you came into my life when I so desperately needed someone. I loved that life at first. I felt so free, like I was created just for this. When I moved down to Littleton to start becoming the real me, to start my journey of becoming the best version of me, real life and real grief over losing Pat set in. I somehow felt unable to forgive myself for ruining a church, a marriage, and someone's else's life. I lost everything: a job, a husband, a house, a church, and friends. I would think about you, but I am not emotionally or mentally ready to even begin to give 100 percent to any relationship. I don't have the capacity to love or even the maturity to make any decision about you or Pat. I feel so young and stuck at this time. I feel so bold, strong, and not accountable to anyone when I start living all on my own. To make my own friends, my own job. It isn't because I don't respect you but living free and alone is the ointment for my soul.

I am so confused right now. I want to keep you as a great friend but also live life just being me. Tater and me! I want to make decisions to empower myself. You are ready and able to give your all to me. I thought I could accept that, but let's face it, I can barely remember where I put my car keys right now. I want this season in my life to be about me, to use this messy situation to become more beautiful, to bring back that zest for life that my soul needs. To grow into who God had created me to be. I am not purposely setting out to hurt you. It is just so hard some days. I just need to live for myself. I am not doing many things right, but I am doing the best I can.

My Letter to Pat

Pat, for two years now I have been saying that I am fried, that I am not only burned out, but that I need to do something different. We would take some time off, and, sure enough, we went right back to where we had been. But I felt that as your best friend and wife that I was to stand by you and support you no matter what. I remember even telling you that I would be there cheering you on. We would come home from a *lunch or dinner with people, and I would say, "It hurts when they constantly tell us what we are doing wrong."*

You always told me, "Collette, people just want to be heard."

I agreed with you and thought that I just needed to love more. I always thought you were a little more spiritual than me, so I tried to love them with all my heart. Then they would leave anonymous letters under your office door complaining about your preaching and it would get me down again. I guess I just wanted everyone to love you like I did. You remain one of the most amazing humans I know, but something is not right in my heart. It took me a week away with my Rainbow Bus friends to realize that I am drowning and losing myself. I no longer am that fun and adventurous woman I so loved. I honestly don't know who I am anymore. But I need the fire back in my soul—I need that confetti! I also need to see if indeed I am in love with Abby or just in love with the life she has. I love you and cherish our deep friendship, but to become the woman I crave to be, the woman who has that gusto for life again, I need to leave you. I need to leave the church, and I no longer desire to be a pastor's wife. If I stay any longer, I will drown.

The next visit to see my counselor I tell her about the letters, but also start describing what I am feeling and going through. I tell her I feel like I have glasses on, and they are covered with Vaseline. I can't see things clearly, I have all this thick skin on, and I want to start peeling away this skin. I mention that some days are so hard, and I just want someone to be kind to me, to smile at me. I don't want people laying on their car horn the moment the traffic light turns green. I most likely have tears in my eyes, and I can't see the light. I don't want the person behind me in the grocery store commenting, "Maybe you should have looked for your wallet before you got to the cashier." I want someone to let me in traffic as I know I am in the wrong lane, but I can't get over. That's what I want—someone to be kind to me.

She keeps encouraging me by slightly leaning forward and nodding ,and at first, I think she wants me to keep giving her examples, but that isn't it.

She finally says, "So, Collette, you want to know how to peel that thick skin away. You want to see with cleared eyes and not look at the world through Vaseline. What do you think you could do?"

All that comes into my mind is Jack Palance in the movie *City Slickers*, where he talks about that *one* thing. I knew it was going to be something like that, that *one* thing. We sit there for a while, just quietly, because I really just want her to tell me. But that isn't how counseling or therapy works, is it? They want you to come up with the answer. And it hit me!

"Yes, I do know how to peel that thick skin away!" It was like layers came off with just me saying it. "*Be. That. Person.*" Be that person that I need. Be that person who will be kind. Be that person who will let someone cut in front of them in traffic. Be that person who waits patiently while someone looks for their wallet.

Twelve years later, it is still my day-to-day pursuit. I don't get it right every day, and I don't do the kind thing. Some days, I am the one honking the horn, yelling, "We use turn signals here in Ohio!" But then, I remember 2009, and I start yelling "Sorry, sorry" out the window. I don't always say the right thing, but I know I will keep getting chances to be that person!

I see her a couple more times. Not once do we ask the question "Am I gay or am I straight?" We talk of things that will change this world. This wasn't a problem to solve; this was a life to live. To be fully alive and fully Collette in hopes of making a small difference in this big world.

QUEEN OF THE BAR

This really is the best of times and the worst of times in my life. I am working this awesome, fun job where I can be myself and get to work race expos and talk to people all day about running. But it is also hard because I get together with Pat and he cries the whole time, and Abby just wants me to come to the mountains when all I really want is to spend time with Tater.

One night, I get home late from work, and I take Tater on a walk. It is dark out, and we decide to just walk up and down Main Street. I hear a lot of laughing and talking coming from one side street, and we walk down and see that it is a bar with its door open. I say, "Tater, let's see if we can go in."

I wave hi to the bartender. "Can my dog come in?"

"Heck yes, bring her in."

Tater and I walk in, and people come over. "Oh, how cute."

"Look at those ears?"

"What is her name?"

"*Tater* is her name!"

One man who maybe has been there a while walks over and says, "My name is George, and I dub you, Tater, Queen of the Bar tonight." He takes her paw and kisses it. "Clear off the bar, everyone. Tater is going to walk on the bar because she is queen."

I am absolutely laughing inside, and I do think Tater is secretly loving this. I pick Tater up and put her on the bar, and darn if she doesn't walk the whole length of it. I turn her around, and she heads back down the bar. The whole time everyone is yelling, "Ta-ter! Ta-ter! Ta-ter!"

When she gets to the end of the bar, I pick her up and put her back on the floor. George comes over and kisses her paw again, and off we go with me yelling, "Bye, everyone. Thanks for making our night."

"Bye, Tater. We love you, Queen Tater!"

I laugh and shake my head the whole way home. I wash her ears off as they smell like beer from dragging them all down the bar.

GRILLING OUT TAKE TWO

Sometime around August of 2010 before I renew my lease, Linda runs from her office and stops me coming out of the elevator. "Collette, we have another building we own just two streets over, so not on Main Street. It is a bottom unit, though. It has a little grassy area and a cement patio. I think Tater would love it there. Hi, Tater. Is that a new bow tie?"

"This sounds so great, Linda."

"It's open right now, go walk over and see it."

"Let's go, Tater!"

Sure enough, it is a cute place and set up just like my apartment now. It even has a little tree that I can tie Tater up to and she can sit in the grass and dream of marrow bones. We head back to see Linda. "Yes, yes, yes, we will take it! Tater loves the grassy area, and I can take my little charcoal grill and set it up right there on that patio."

"Oh, Collette, we can only do gas grills at that place."

Hehehehahahahohoho, you're killing me, Linda!

SATURDAY TONY'S RUN

December 2010—my manager, Amanda, and I meet with a person from Tony's Meat Market. It is an old Italian fresh market that sells hand-cut meats, produce, old-fashioned candy, baked goods, and other grocery items a half mile from BRC. They say, "We would like to start a run group from our store. Would you be interested in partnering with us? We could start it one Saturday a month and see how it goes. We will make breakfast burritos for everyone who comes, and they can get discounts on anything they buy."

To me, it sounds perfect as I love Tony's Meat Market. Amanda agrees! We would love to.

"OK," they say. "Let's have the first one on January 1st."

My eyes get wide. "You want to start a run group on January 1st at 7:30 in the morning?"

"Yes. What do you think?"

"Well, for me it works because I will probably be in bed by nine, but I wonder if other people do things on NYE?"

But even if we have two people come, it will be a success, so we say yes! Nellie says she will help. We end up having forty-five people that January 1st, so we decide to just do the run every Saturday.

BE. THAT. PERSON.

Trying to describe what this Saturday Tony's Run means to me is almost impossible. It is like having a big family reunion every week. New people join in, and we have runners, walkers, hikers, adults, kids, teens, dogs, kids on bikes, kids in strollers, old and young all gathered to do a three-mile loop and at the end sit around eating breakfast burritos and feeling good about starting the weekend with friends. If you are new, we make sure someone shows you the course. We have a raffle every week of random, crazy things we would find around BRC.

You come ten times; you get a shirt. One hundred times, you get a special shirt. We have a water stop set up around mile two, and this water stop is pretty much what I was created for. I yell and cheer as I see people coming and hand out high fives and hugs for making it to the water stop. They stop, we chat a little bit, and off they go to finish and off I go to cheer for the next little group. It is the highlight of my week. It is fun and encouraging.

No one cares if you run fast or if you walk. If you come once or two hundred times, you are family. Friendships were made here that are still going strong. When kids come, they get this small punch card, and for every three miles, we punch out the miles. After they complete a marathon, 26.2 miles (we rounded up to twenty-seven as that is divisible by three), we make this long paper finish line that they run through with everyone there yelling and hollering. It really is my family.

We dress up for all the holidays and hand out prizes for best dressed. We hide plastic Easter eggs at the water stop at Easter. At Thanksgiving, we all dress up as turkeys or pilgrims, and friends even came as mashed potatoes and pie one year. At Christmas, we all wear Santa hats. When the Denver Broncos are in the Super Bowl, people wear jerseys. On St. Patty's Day, we chase a crazy friend of mine dressed as a leprechaun and handing out candy. We make sure that everyone says hi to someone they don't know just in case they need a smile or someone to just be nice to them that day.

My favorite is when people bring family members from out of town who are visiting. We see them a couple times a year, and it really is like a family union, getting all caught up on the last six months. I am still friends with some of these out-of-town family members on social media.

As with life and any family, we also have to share in the sorrow of losing one of our most consistent runners. Deb and Dean are always so supportive and make new people feel welcome. When Dean dies, it hits us all. A group of us from Tony's run go to his funeral to celebrate his life and to be there for Deb.

Deb remains not only a great friend of mine, but a great human. She has been one of the biggest cheerleaders for me in the writing of this book.

We will see people through divorces, people moving away, people getting married, and grandkids being born. One guy trained to through-hike the Appalachian Trail and showed up with his backpack and hiking boots, and guess what? He did it! Every Saturday I think still of that group and miss that family, and my heart swells with happiness that for five years, I got to experience life with people who made my soul big.

One of our Saturday Tony's Runs

A BIG MOMENT!

Also December 2010—I am tossing and turning and look at the clock. It is almost midnight. I have always been a great sleeper, but this last year has been tough on my sleeping. I get Tater up to tell her we have to go on a walk. If she thinks it is weird, she doesn't say. We aren't going for just a walk; we are headed to the big blue mailbox on the corner of the street. I grab the manila envelope on our way out. No one else is out, we get to the collection box, and I open the chute and close it. I open it again and again but don't put the manila envelope in. Tater finally looks up at me to say, "Did you wake me up just to open and close this blue mailbox?"

The next time, I open it and drop the envelope in. I sit next to the box and start crying. Tater sits right next to me with her head on my lap. I don't know how long I sit there and cry. Tater looks up at me, and I say, "I just mailed off our divorce papers. You see, Tater, I have felt so stuck lately. Like I wasn't moving forward or backward, just buffering like a computer does when it is stuck or looking for service. I decided I actually have to do something to move me forward. I don't know what the future holds for me, but I can't stay stuck." Tater seems to move a little closer to me and the moon peeps out from the clouds.

" Pat and I filled out the paperwork...We don't have children, but we both agree that you are my dog. I get you, and he gets our credit cards! Oh, Tater, life seems so confusing right now. But let's see how this all plays out. People just think that because I am the one leaving that it isn't hard, but it is hard."

Yes, I left a husband, a church, a job, a house, and lost tons of friends because of it, but I feel like my soul stopped buffering and found its internet connection when I finally dropped that envelope in the box.

April 2011—I get another manila envelope in the mail. This one makes our divorce final. Abby told me to call her when I was divorced, but I don't call her. I call one of my running friends who lives close by. She comes over with beer, and I don't think I say two words. She doesn't push it and sits there with me until I head to bed. Before I lie down, I ask God, "God, are you going to spit on me because I fell in love with a woman, and I am now divorced?"

It is so quiet, but I get no response no from God. In the middle of the night, I feel someone playing with my hair. It isn't a dream, but I'm not awake either, if that makes sense. It feels so great, like someone is just running my hair through their fingers. I do wake up to see if someone has come into my bedroom, but no one is there. I hear a whisper, though: "Collette, I love you and you are going to be OK. We have soul confetti to throw around!"

Thanks, God!

I wake the next morning sad, but unhindered, heavy and light all at once.

ANOTHER LOSS, ANOTHER BIG DECISION

2011—My divorce is final, and you perhaps wonder if I then ride off into the sunset with Abby and live happily ever after. I do not. This last year and a half has been erratic, unbalanced, and confusing, but I was embarking on a do-over, if you will. I wasn't hoping my heart changed—I was hoping my heart blossomed. This is such an exciting time for me, making new friends, living in a new city, working my dream job, running trails with friends and with Tater, but I'm also dealing with heavy, hurtful emails and people randomly stopping by my work. Another person came by last week to tell me of a group from her church that gets together that maybe I would like to be a part of. They meet once a week and talk about how they can stop being gay. I have to wade through all these emotions, all these great and heavy things, and keep my focus on discovering me. To become that vibrant woman I was created to be. To rethink how I impact others and the world around me. To look at people with new eyes and no thick skin. To be full of compassion. To treat others how I would like to be treated. To come out of this filled with all those passions and dreams I have and to radiate love, courage, and acceptance to the world around me. To do all this, to use this to bring Collette back spunkier than ever, it will take another loss.

My relationship with Abby won't help in this quest. I loved her, she taught me how to be a great friend, and we had so many fun times together. I will always think of her in terms of miles:

- the miles we ran together with our dogs.

- the miles we mountain biked.

- the miles we cross country skied

- however many miles it takes to fly to Key West

- and the number of texts we sent to each other would add up to be all these miles combined.

However, it is becoming so clear to me that I love being and I love living free from any romantic relationship. This is who I am. I like having strong bonds with people, and I love connecting to loads of friends, but at the end of the day, I love it being Collette and Tater. It's who I am, and I am finally realizing that it is OK. It isn't selfish, it is being me, fully me. Still today, I feel this same way. I am more myself when I live free from any romantic relationship. It makes me fully Collette!

GRIEF AND GRAND OPENINGS

I am realizing that life seems to be made up of joys and sorrows. They both live in my heart together. I am grieving over the loss of Abby, but at the same time, life has some fun, magical moments. I think life was always like this, but I would some how cover up the sorrows or ignore them, put on that thick skin, and just pay attention to all the joys. I realize now, life is fully lived when I allow these two to hang out in my soul together. For instance....

I love grand openings!

A new grocery store opening is a special event for me, and I have made it a quest to go to as many as possible. One year, in Fraser, Colorado, a small grocery store was closing, and a brand new one was opening right across the street. I don't know what I liked more: the old store closing or the new one opening. The employees would move what they could ,or rather, what was allowed to be moved, in the new store overnight. All the fresh fruits, veggies, produce, breads, and so on that weren't allowed to be moved got sold off super cheap. I arrived for the closing around 7:00 p.m. They get on the loudspeaker and announce:

"Hurry to the produce section. All cabbages are a nickel."

"All donuts are a dollar a dozen!"

"Come grab eggs for ten cents!"

It is all so unbelievable.

When the new store opens, there I am in line at 6:00 a.m. to partake in the grand opening—a free loaf of bread and a gift card to the first one hundred people. Cupcakes and balloons just add to the fun. Each department has samples, and I don't think I need to eat for two days after.

A grand opening at the Kroger near my place in Cincinnati included a high school marching band and lots of TV stations. I will have to say, however, the best grand opening happened at a McDonald's right up the street from me in Littleton, Colorado.

McDonald's had sent out a postcard to all the apartments and homes in the area and it said, "We have remodeled our McDonald's. Come to the grand opening November 22nd, 2011. First one hundred people will get one free value meal every week for a year!"

I tell Tater we absolutely cannot miss it. That morning we get up and head to the McDonald's before 6:00 a.m. to have a chance at being in the first one hundred. When we arrive, however, the whole place is dark, and no one is in line. I check the postcard to make sure it is the right date. We walk up to the main door, and there is a sign on the door: "Sorry for the inconvenience. We did not get our permit in time to open today. If you call this number, you can find out if you are one of the first one hundred." I call right then, and a manager comes to the door. We are indeed one of the first one hundred! I can't believe it. Tater and I are whooping and hollering. We are told to come back tomorrow to pick up our winning postcard. That whole year is a blast. Each week, I get a free sandwich, fries, and a drink. Some days, I pick it up and take it to work and share with whoever is working. If I go out of town, I give it to a friend to use. Some days, I get the meal and hand it to my homeless friend who stands at the corner. It is the coolest thing!

How fun is this punch card?

2012 IS BEYOND EPIC!

2012 seems to be a pretty epic year for me. I turned fifty years old in December of 2011, and it has been a dream of mine to run the Big Sur Marathon in California. Amanda, my manager, and one of our shoe reps make that dream come true. They get me a comp into the race. I can't believe it! I start training. A bunch of my friends join me each week on my long runs. The info you get from the marathon suggests training on hills and then to add more hills to your training. Since the trails are sometimes too snow-packed, we run on this hilly dirt road out in the hinterlands. It is actually super fun. It is a straight road but a hilly one. One long run, we have to tack on more miles than just the road as I need to get in eighteen miles. There is an off-road trail nearby, so we run that as well. We are about sixteen miles into the run, and I am not sure I can finish. A friend we call Crazy Chris is running with me (he is also the one who dresses as a leprechaun on St. Patrick's Day for our Tony's Run). I tell him I need to stop and just walk the last two miles as absolutely everything on me hurts. He is an ultra-runner and used to this kind of talk. He says, "Do your eyebrows hurt?"

"Ummm, no."

"Do your elbows hurt?"

"No, I guess those don't hurt either."

"Well then, everything doesn't hurt."

"By gosh, you are right!"

We end up running the last two miles.

The training is all done, and I have never felt more in shape and ready for a race. I take off on my road trip to the marathon. I pack my Subaru up with my usual tent, sleeping bag, cooler filled with beer, and my journal. I also put my mountain bike in the car just in case. I wasn't even this excited for my first marathon. Paula and Liz are going to come out to watch me finish and help get me where I need to be to catch the shuttle to the start line. My best friend from college, Kate, is driving down from San Francisco as well. I have six CDs that friends have made for me, but I bring a Jimmy Buffet cassette tape too.

If I thought the training was fun, the marathon is that much better. They have closed Highway 1 to only the runners, so Paula and Liz drop me off to catch a 3:30 a.m. bus (yes, they do this for me because of their big souls!). This bus will drive us to the start line in Big Sur. 26.2 miles later, we will end in Carmel. I tell them I will see them at mile twenty-five, the first place spectators are allowed. I have a couple cups of coffee and some Gatorade, I sit down in the bus, and this friendly chap sits next to me. He tells me he is from San Luis Obispo. He keeps saying, "Not Saint Louis, *San Luis*." He keeps repeating it over and over. It is pretty funny.

It is an hour-long drive, it is dark, and you can see stars and a little bit of the course. All of a sudden, I have to pee. Like it is hurting so badly. I can't even think. I turn to my new friend next to me from San Luis Obispo and say, "I have to pee so badly. What am I going to do?"

He replies, "I don't know, but I know what you *aren't* going to do!"

We finally get to the start line but pass it right by. The driver announces that we must turn around about five minutes down the road. I am a wreck. We finally stop as we pull up to the start line, and everyone is yelling, "Let her out, let her go first, let her out!" It is hilarious. I run to the porta john!

I find a place to sit on the sidewalk to wait for the start and others join me. I talk to people and sit there looking at everyone's running shoes—because that is what I love doing, seeing what shoes people are wearing. Start time is

6:45 a.m., and we start lining up at about 6:15. We sing the national anthem, and then they release all these doves. I am a crying mess; it is so beautiful.

We start heading downhill into deep redwood forest. Even though I stop to pee three more times, I really get into a groove. At mile five, my foot starts hurting. I take some ibuprofen, and from then on, there is nothing else that bugs, bothers, or is even an issue. My clothes aren't bugging me, my hydration pack is great, nothing is rubbing. It is just perfect.

At about mile nine, we start heading down this huge hill, and you can hear these drummers. Banging and banging. It isn't drums like in a band. It is a much deeper sound, and when I turn the corner, there are these huge drums, like as tall as I am. Twenty-five of them, and mostly women playing them. I am crying because it is so amazing. *Then* I turn this other corner and start up, up, up, and you can see how far it will be. The wind is cold and just hitting your face because now we are heading straight toward the Pacific Ocean. I am holding on to my hat as it keeps blowing off, and I am trying to run as much as I can but walking a lot to save energy. No one is speaking—at least I can't hear anyone until a guy comes right next to me and says, "Now you know why they call it Hurricane Point."

I now realize why they say to train on hills. You get to the top, and you are spent. Most of us just stop and look at the ocean. But then I start hearing something that sounds magnificent, and I head toward the sound and realize I am now running on the most photographed bridge in California, the Bixby Bridge. I keep hearing this passionate music, and I start crying again, as I can see where this music is coming from. There on this concrete wonder is a man in a tuxedo playing this grand piano. It floors me! I can't believe I get to experience all this.

More and more hills, but at mile twenty-one, someone is handing out strawberries at the water stop. Finally at mile twenty-five, I can see Liz, and she is filming. Paula is at the top of the hill, and I am telling everyone, "Don't stop, keep running to go see Paula."

They keep running but ask, "Who's Paula?"

"My amazing friend!"

I get to the finish line, and there is Kate waiting to hug me and hand me a beer. The medals they give you are these homemade ones, and I have mine around my neck as we head to get breakfast burritos and Longboard beers. I sit down at the table and knock this new amazing medal into the side of the table, and it breaks in half. Everyone asks if I want them to go exchange it. Nope, this broken medal is absolutely perfect.

The finish of Big Sur Marathon before I broke the medal.

That night Kate and I sit in the hotel lobby in these huge comfy wraparound chairs and drink two bottles of wine, overlooking the Pacific Ocean and talking and catching up. I feel so light and free like I don't want this day to end.

The four of us meet up for breakfast the next morning. They take off to head home, and I head south down the coast to camp along the water for the next week. I have no words to describe how amazing this trip is. I drive three thousand miles, and my final campsite is in Green River, Utah. I arrive in the dark and put my tent up. I am so giddy, excited, and tired that when I wake up the next day, I see I put the tent poles in the wrong way. Pat and Tater are at my place to greet me when I get home with a big welcome home sign and a cold beer.

STORE MANAGER

September 2012—Another epic event in my life! I become the store manager!

My manager, Amanda, will take a different job within the company and promotes me to store manager of Boulder Running Company, Littleton. Yes, nine years after I walked into BRC and felt at home, I am now the manager. As with my life and with managing, it is hard and challenging and a blast and a kick in the pants and eye-opening. It stretches me and is exactly what I need to become spunky Collette again. I didn't have it dialed in, but, wow, I loved it. I would say I am gregarious, and others would say over the top and loud. I don't always do or say the right thing, and I am challenged with boundaries. You see, it really is my dream job, and I am ecstatic. I think of it pretty much twenty-four seven. I absolutely love it. I run with Tater at 7:00 a.m. and think of something fun we can do at the store. I stop right there and text people about the idea. Yes, at 7:00 a.m.!

But even with all these growing pains I was having, when I think back on my time as manager, I think of all the *amazing*, incredible times that I had. I loved the staff! They were my family, and that probably was the reason I felt I could just be myself. This brought on some epic fails as well as some tremendous wins.

I truly believe that a business will be successful and make money by being kind to people. I yearn to make BRC the *Cheers* of running stores— "Where everybody knows your name, and we're always glad you came." I love when customers come in and say, "Hi, just on my lunch break, and I wanted to stop in to say a hearty hello!" and "I'm not here to buy anything, just was in the neighborhood."

Amanda lets me promote an amazing young man to be the assistant manager. His name is Benny. He is another quiet soul who understands kindness and treating others how he wants to be treated. I end up going to cheer him on in so many races and cheer for him in day-to-day life. We make a great team. These years are filled with some of the best days of my life, even during some of the usual interpersonal problems that came up.

We have sooooo many things always going on at the store. Because we want to be more than a running store, not everything is about running. We show movies at the store, yes, like *ET*, *Sandlot*, or *Casper*. We provide popcorn and Raisinets, and people provide their own chairs. On Memorial Day, we grill out hot dogs. On July 4th, we hand out slices of apple pie. We have pumpkin carving contests and Peeps diorama contests. At Christmas, I dress as Mrs. Claus, and Benny is so talented that he does awesome videos for the twelve days of Christmas. We have a men's night.

Runs—boy, we offer runs. We have trail runs, Tony's Runs, speed workouts, a race team, training groups, a walking group, poker runs (you get a playing card at each half mile and the person with the best poker hand wins a prize), photo scavenger runs, and bingo card runs. For Thanksgiving, we work the local Turkey Trot water stop right outside the store. We use the store for yoga, weight loss class, and Zumba. The highlight of every year for me, though, is our *Diva Night*. This isn't just a lady's night; this is *Diva Night*. I asked one of my favorite customers to describe Diva Night as I would just keep saying, "It was the best, it was awesome." Here is what she sent me:

"Anyone who is a customer of Boulder Running Company knows about Diva Night. It is the one night where women come together...all shapes and sizes, all levels of fitness. All hoping to win a prize, sample some goods, watch a fashion show, do a short fun run, and win a prize. If you didn't win a prize, you root for the other gals who did win. The bigger the prize, the more excited you get. Not only for yourself, but for everyone. In reality, Diva Night is a brilliant marketing tool to showcase products, appreciate clientele, and increase sales, but for we gals who enjoy going to it, we see it as an absolutely fun night of laughter, merriment, and bonding. Lining up at 2:00 p.m. for a party that doesn't start until seven—crazy! But so worth it. The fun starts then. When the ringleader comes out in a coconut shell bra, grass skirt, and tiara, you know it is going to be a fun night."

The night ends with someone being crowned Miss Diva, and she receives a head-to-toe outfit complete with hat, sunglasses, shirt, bra, pants, socks, and shoes. I hand her the tiara off my head, but not my coconut shell bra. It was months to get ready for and a year to recover.

The awesome staff after one Diva Night.

Every day, I loved going to work. The staff during my years at the store was everything you dream of. We were all different yet felt the same. We all had different gifts, talents, and personalities, but together we made a great family.

ME, I BUY A HOUSE!

I meet Anna my first year at BRC. She is another one of those big souled people. She is a part of our running groups as well as someone who always stopped in the store to say hi, and she even ends up working there. She brings her husband to our Saturday Tony's Runs. He is a funny, witty realtor. His name is Greg. He asks me one day, "Collette, why are you still renting?"

I give some answer about how I like that maintenance always comes and fixes things and other things like that. What I don't tell him is that for six months now, I have been drawing the perfect house for Tater and me. I show Tater and she says, "You have to believe!"

I am content in my apartment, but I really want a fenced backyard and a big ol' kitchen to cook in. And so, it started. I will spare you the details of some of the houses we look at. One day, I am at work, and I get a text from Greg: "Call me!"

I call right away.

"I found your house, but you have to get here right away."

I am still on a slide phone, so he gives me directions, and off I go. I pull into the driveway, and I gasp. It is the little box house just like I have been drawing. I already know what the inside will look like. Indeed, it was eight hundred square feet of pure magic. I walk in, and it's old wood floors with a big open kitchen, a big fenced-in backyard, a deep old bathtub, and two small bedrooms connected by a closet that you can walk through to get to the other bedroom. It is located in the city and county of Denver.

I declare, "It is the cutest house on the planet!" From this day on, it will be called C. H. O. P. I put an offer in, and they accept. Now comes the hard part; the waiting, the inspections, the financial part, and everything else that may block my dream. I take Tater over there all the time to walk around the house and sit out back. I leave one of her marrow bones there so it will be her home for real. Things are moving along, and then the financial part comes. I have no money for a down payment and really have no money at all. But I get the loan. I keep asking Greg, "Someone's going to loan me money? A bank is really going to give me money?"

"Yes, they are, but please don't say that at the closing!"

We get a closing date, and I am so giddy I can barely sleep. I keep telling Tater that dreams really do come true if we just believe. I have my apartment all boxed up, ready to move, as the closing day is the next day. Wow! What a thrill! I can barely sleep, and I just am so flipping excited.

Greg calls around noon and says the closing has been pushed back to the next week. I start crying. I mean, I know it is happening, but I was all set to spend the night and pop my prosecco! Now I must live out of boxes for a week, which compared to 2009, seems OK.

I end up closing the day before Thanksgiving, November 21, 2012. It really is one of the happiest days of my life. Pat and a handful of other awesome friends help me move everything and even help me unpack. Greg and Anna buy me a new toilet as a housewarming present, my running buddies buy me a cool beanbag sofa/chair, other friends give me their top-of-the-line washer and dryer, and Pat puts in a doggie door and builds this over-sized awesome Adirondack chair and paints it yellow. It is big enough for two people and one dog.

When I go back and reread my journal from this point on, I have soooo many entries that say over and over, "I love this house!" and "I am so grateful for this house!"

And Greg was right. I pay less in mortgage than I did renting. Find you a good realtor with a big soul.

The Cutest House on the Planet!

OFF ON ROAD TRIPS

Camping across the US and going on road trips may just seem like chapters in this book, but I am finding that road trips really are a part of my DNA, something that brings a shine back to my soul. An article in *Elite Daily* says this: "People who go on road trips are spontaneous, optimistic, and wise." Ha!

While my fear of flying is over, I still prefer to just pack my car and take off. I don't have to wait for an announcement that the seat belt sign is off, and I can now move freely about the cabin and go to the bathroom. I can pull over anytime I want. If I take my shoes off, it isn't to run them through a scanner. And, really, if I wanted to, I could pack knitting needles and a Swiss army knife. (Although I don't have any more knives as TSA has taken all mine away because I always forget I have one in my backpack.)

Driving in a car helps me dream and discover. It empties my head and fills my head all at the same time. So as I become more Collette, I start going on road trips again. As back in 1986, I pack my tent, sleeping bag, books, a cooler filled with beer, and my journal. I take many trips back to see my family in Ohio. It is always so fun to stop and camp the first night and pull into my mom's house tired and ready to stay up until 2:00 a.m. playing Back Alley Bridge. These trips are filled with spending time with my mom, two sisters, my brother, and his wife and always a trip to Kelly's Island by ferry.

BE. THAT. PERSON.

When I take off to head back to Colorado, I end up calling my mom thirteen times within fifty miles to tell her how much I love her. There isn't a rest stop on I-70 I haven't been to. In Iowa, no matter what time it is, I stop for a Maid-Rite sandwich or two. If there is a big truck stop, I pull in and buy some trinket or some funny bumper sticker. When I pull into Denver, Pat and Tater are always waiting outside the Cutest House on the Planet with a fun sign. Pat has also either done some epic paint job, or hung fun lights, or generally made my house more awesome while I was away.

I end up traveling to California twice, once for the Big Sur Marathon and another time for the Club Skirts Dinah Shore Weekend in Palm Springs. I don't see any golf, but I attend every pool party and see Natasha Bedingfield in concert. I stay with Paula and Liz. They remain good friends and a constant reminder of generosity. They really understand spreading their soul confetti.

I take one road trip, however, that really brings back my shine.

I take off for Arizona, just me and my car packed with the usual. I leave in the early morning, and there is just a sliver of moon out. I start heading south. I cross over the Arizona state line and start driving up mountains. I start noticing signs that say, "Caution, winter driving conditions." I actually laugh. But sure enough, I hit snow—but not for long as I start heading down to high, dry desert. I am headed to a KOA campground in Apache Junction so I can spend one week running all over the Superstition Mountains.

My first day, I drive on a washboard, potholed dirt road seven miles back from the highway. I arrive at the trailhead, and a group of ladies are looking at a big wooden map of the mountains. I ask them where the best trail for running would be.

" You can't run here."

" Shoot, it isn't allowed?"

"Oh, it's allowed, it's just too rocky!"

"I will take that into consideration." I, in fact, do not take that into consideration. I take off up a trail that leads to a saddle that leads to a rock outcropping that leads to me breathing hard but in awe. There I stand, looking out at miles of cactus and yell loudly, "*I love my life!*" It looks like all the cactus trees are waving back saying, "*You go, girl!*" I head back down and find a local lunch spot, go back to the campground, and sit poolside to read, journal, and have a beer. Each new day, a new trail, a new vista, and the same declaration to the cacti.

The cacti cheering for me!

I call Pat—still with a flip phone!—to ask him to find me a Whole Foods or something of the sort as I want to make a cheese platter for dinner, and I can't do cow's milk. He texts me directions, and off I go, but on the way, I find an In-N-Out Burger. Hallelujah! Since I had been to one in California, I couldn't wait to go again. My journal says, "They are the best burgers I have ever had." Then two pages later, on my trip home, I am driving through Grants, New Mexico, and stop at what looks like a roadside diner made just for me. It's called Blake's Lotaburger. I now attest that these burgers are the best, and no more needs to be said on the subject.

I must have been absolutely lovesick with these burgers because not long after that, my low gas light comes on. I decide to pull over at the next exit, but the next exit doesn't have any gas stations, and my flip phone can't help me find any. I keep driving, and now my car isn't saying thirty-two miles until empty anymore. It just says, "LO." I keep driving, hoping for an exit. Now my LO light goes off. My heart is pounding. There is a rest stop, and I wonder whether to keep driving and hope, or to pull over and ask people. I pull over, park, and jump out of my car. I run up to an older gentleman and tell him my story. I am speaking so fast as I assume talking fast makes the situation more dire.

"There is gas at the next exit, but it is five miles away."

Another man has overheard everything and comes over. They decide that one of them will lead the way and the other one will drive behind me in case I run out of gas. If I do, they will pick me up to take me to get gas. It sounds like a great plan. Off we go! Soon enough, I see the exit, and as I am pulling over, I am beeping my horn and yelling out the window. They are beeping their horns and yelling as well. We are whooping, "Yay, yay, yay!" The one guy in front of me pulls off with me to make sure I am OK and even asks if I have enough money for gas. He and I both go into the store to pay, and we tell the cashier the whole story.

My heart is so full when I get back into my car, and I realize I am crying—with relief for not running out of gas, but mostly for gratitude. I can't believe that two strangers helped me, that two strangers shared a little bit of their soul confetti with me. I grab my journal and write the one man's name down so I will never forget. His name was Jeb Robertson. If you read this book, or if anyone knows him, please tell him his kindness still has a special place in my heart.

When I pull into my driveway, there are Tater and Pat with a cute sign, ice-cold beer, and a newly painted living room.

PERKS OF BEING A RUNNING STORE MANAGER

I fly into Atlanta and get into the airport, and there is a person holding a sign with my name on it. It is starting out to be a great week. When I get into my hotel room, in the middle of the king-size bed filled with down pillows is a large black carry-on soft suitcase with my name embroidered on it. Inside is a pair of new shoes and running apparel for any weather conditions. Yes, indeed, I have arrived at Mizuno Dendoshi, a way for the Mizuno brand to share their story and get us on board with what is coming next for the Mizuno company. How it works is they tell us, and we tell the customers. The week is filled with group runs, group talks, group meals, and group groups, all in a beautiful, lush setting. The Mizuno company makes us managers feel a part of something exciting. I feel pampered all week, and I still use that black carry-on.

I have the same type of experience with the Nike brand. This time, I fly into their main campus in Portland, Oregon, and a limo ride to a fun hotel to spend a week learning and sharing. Every day we receive a new pair of shoes, but my journal goes into minute detail of all the food and restaurants that they spoiled us with. The week ends with Nike paying for us to run the epic two-hundred-mile Hood to Coast Relay. It is fun if you like running at 1:00 a.m. with a headlamp, sleeping in a van for two days with sweaty clothes, and drinking a beer at the finish line on the beach at 9:00 a.m. I do indeed love all that.

And yet another awesome part of being a store manager: at one point, I count one hundred pairs of new shoes in my closet. It really is a dream job for me. It remains the job that used my passions, gifts, talents, and personality traits (both good and bad) more than any other job.

INSTAGRAM

July 15, 2015—I make my first Instagram post. Why is this such a big deal? Well, first off because I finally have an Android phone. Yep, I traded in my flip phone. But, much more important than that is I will end up making another whole family of friends. I will meet people from all over the world who have basset hounds, or love basset hounds, or who are just crazy dog people. These folks will end up being my clan. They understand that a dog is more than a dog, that, yes, we cancel outings to stay home with our hounds because we worked all day and couldn't possibly go out again. I text a handful of these people every single day. If I liked talking on the phone, Cathy Jo would want to talk every day. I haven't met 90 percent of these people, but I feel so connected to them. I can't explain it, but I love it. They will see me through great times and difficult times. I will encourage and cheer for them, and we have a bond that is strong and healthy. We really pull together when one of these amazing dogs goes to the Rainbow Bridge. We feel the grief like it is our own.

I love my Instagram family. When we comment on each other's posts, we aren't just saying, "Oh, how cute." We are saying, "Happy Monday, dear friend. Hope it's a good one. Thinking of you." We are there for each other. Yes, when I get that VW van, I will take off and meet all these wonderful, big souled humans and their wonderful and big souled dogs. Some, like my awesome friend Tracy, live across the pond, so I will have to make my way there as well. I am one of those strange people who love social media.

SPUNKY COLLETTE

There is a change happening in my heart and my life. I am feeling like me again, like I am blooming. I compare it to having a jack-in-the-box in my soul. I was turning the arm over and over, and instead of a funny stuffed animal coming out, finally it went *pop* and out came confetti. Confetti people had given me over the years. My passions are blooming, and even though there are still some tough times, I feel alive again. I am finding out that I love running, but most importantly, I love running with people, getting groups of people together for a trail run to talk and take pictures and laugh and hear about each other's weeks and sometimes even cry. I am finding I love cheering for people on a racecourse almost more than running any race. I encourage them during training, and then I go to watch them finish the race.

My friend Andy (remember him, wouldn't be my maid of honor) lives in Denver as well now. In fact, his partner at this time is the food editor for the *Denver Post,* and I am perhaps his biggest fan. When Andy tells me his name, my eyes pop out. I am starstruck when I finally meet him. Andy lives on mile twenty-one of the Rock and Roll Denver Marathon. I go watch the start of the half marathon and cheer at mile six for those people and then drive over to Andy's house. We sit in lawn chairs outside drinking Bloody Marys and eating these amazing brunch items, rooting and cheering for everyone that comes through. So many times, I hear, "You sold me my shoes!" It makes my day to hand out big high fives and tell them they look great!

Another great thing developing in my life is how amazing my relationship with Pat is. No, it isn't a romantic let's-get-married-again thing. It is much deeper than that. Not everyone understands how we aren't romantically involved, but our friendship is full of trust, loyalty, and respect. We are free to be ourselves. We always use the line from *Rudolph the Red Nosed Reindeer:* "We are independent, together!" You see, he never went back to being a pastor and instead moved down to Denver as well to eventually do things he got a kick out of. He spends years refereeing ice hockey games, but his real passion is animals and helping people. He becomes a house, ranch, dog, cat, horse, you name it sitter. He understands animals better than I understand baseball! He also continues to do many weddings. My soul feels bright yellow right now, and little do I know that it is time for another challenge.

BUCKET

I met Steve not long after I moved down to Denver. I was in the middle of searching for breath, beauty, and God. Our manager at the time said, "We have a new person starting today. His name is Steve, and he can't work weekends. But you will love him."

I thought, *Wow, he must be pretty good as not working weekends in a customer service industry is pretty big.*

Steve walks into the store and comes right over to introduce himself. I swear his eyes sparkle, and he has a huggable aura about him. I like him on the spot.

A couple days later at work, he and I are in the back room, and he says, "Collette, what's your story?"

My heart drops into my belly button. I stammer, "Ummmmmm, I haven't told anyone here my story. I just can't yet as you may make judgments like others do."

"Oh, try me!"

"OK, well, I was married—wait, I am still married—to a really great guy. He is a pastor and has been for fifteen years, so that made me a pastor's wife. I found myself drowning and developing thick skin, which I don't like. I may be in love with a woman. So, it was suggested that I move down to Denver so the church could heal and move on and so I can find me again. People from the church seem to email me and even stop down here sometimes to tell me that I make them sick to their stomachs. I want to come out of this experience with a huge soul and a love for people so if they ever go through something like this, I can help them. I want to make something beautiful out of what now seems to be more than I can handle. It seems like Pat is the only one who still seems to love me. So here I am. I don't need to be fixed. I just need a friend."

"I'll be your friend, Collette!"

My journal doesn't say it, but I know I cry and hug him.

Then I ask him, "Why can't you work weekends?"

"My wife travels all week, and I like to be home when she comes back from a long work week."

Again, my journal doesn't say it, but I know I cry. A couple of days after all this, I am trying to tell Steve about a gal who came back into the store that he had fit for a pair of shoes. I am describing her, and I say, "You know, what's her bucket!"

He says, "What's her bucket?" and starts howling. From that moment on, Steve is called Bucket. He calls me Bucket too.

We go to brunch or breakfast at least once a week. If I go on a run near his house, he meets me after for a burger and maybe a Bloody Mary. We get burritos or margaritas. He comes over to my place, and I cook while he sits and pets Tater all night. He and his wife have a Jack Russell named Ely. So he is a dog lover.

Weekends, though, are saved for his wife. I can't wait to hear what they have to eat as they love great food. They spend their weekends cooking or going out to one of their local favorite restaurants. If his wife is in town, she comes into the store and gets some crazy colored shoes and a fun outfit. They travel all over the world, and I keep telling Bucket that I am going to travel again and someday travel in a yellow VW van. He, Pat, and I go to baseball and hockey games. We are family. I love how we just talk and talk and share, he listens, and I try not to hog the conversation.

He sends postcards when he and his wife go somewhere. They bring me back this gorgeous pashmina from one trip. He never judges me, and he listens no matter what crazy ideas or nutso event I am going through. When I become store manager, he is my sounding board. We are best buds!

Things are awesome and amazing until prostate cancer comes knocking at his door. I sit with him during his chemo treatments, and we laugh and cry. He is a favorite of all the nurses there, probably because of his huggable aura. On his last treatment, all of us from the store make a big cheesy poster congratulating him. He tries coming back to work, and it seems to be going smoothly until cancer all over his body doesn't just knock at his door, but swings the door wide open and charges right in.

We celebrate his sixtieth birthday by going out for pizza. He gets to work a couple more days on and off for short spurts. When he works, things seemed calmer, more peaceful, and definitely more fun. Some days he gets so tired he has to sit on the treadmill and rest. Some days, he has to call in sick, and one day he has to leave work because he has no control over his bowels.

One weekend, he, his wife, and I go on a mountain bike ride. It is his first ride in over two years. Sure, he gets tired, but we have a blast. Two weeks later, he calls to tell me the doctors think he has six to eight months left to live. I am unsure what I will do without this kindred soul. So many of my journal entries say, "I miss Bucket at work." In late September, he comes over to my house for dinner. I make chicken schnitzel, spaetzle, and homemade apple-sauce. And guess what? We have a blast!

On Tuesday, November 11, his wife calls me to tell me that on Saturday she will move Steve into hospice. Pat and I drive up to see him one last time at his house. It is snowing so badly, and Pat's car is sliding all over. We also need the code to open the gate to their neighborhood. I call Bucket's house from the gate phone and my coworker Donna, is there already and answers. I am a wreck and shrieking, "We need the code for the gate." I start crying for many reasons, the least being that we don't have the code. We finally get to his house. I lie next to him on their bed and read him a letter I have written, and I sit there sobbing and reading it. He isn't really aware of it, but it sure does my heart wonders. I tell him all the things I love about him and how he helped me through a dark night of my soul with no judgment and never once said, "Collette, enough, just move on!" Nope, he was all about love and making others feel safe and valued. We all leave, and I tell his wife I will stop by the hospice place on Saturday after work.

Saturday, November 15, 2014

I get to our Saturday Tony's Run at 7:00 a.m. to start getting things set up. I get a text at 7:15 a.m. from Bucket's sister that says, "He has passed." He never made it to hospice, and now I can't even think or function. I text Donna, my friend from work, to tell her, and I head to her house to shower. We then head to Bucket's house, and, sure enough, there he is on the bed, mouth wide open and clearly dead. I cry and weep, and I head home.

It snows all day, and I now start a new way of living without my friend. As I watch the snow come down, I realize I have now come full circle. I am once again searching for breath, beauty, and God. *However*, this time my bighearted, steadfast companion has left me a blueprint on how to Be. That. Person.

Bucket and me!

I AM NOT GREAT AT METRICS

I still love walking in the doors at work even though my soul is splintered, and I am learning to live with both joy and grief. I miss so much about Bucket and work seems different. I don't feel as confident without Bucket there encouraging me and telling me I don't have to have it dialed it.

Early on when I became the manager, BRC gets bought out by a family that owns many sport stores and real estate in Colorado called the Gart Brothers. I'm not against the buyout. Yes, I love the original owners of BRC and believe in their business concept, but I really do understand wanting to sell it. They made it awesome, and it is time to move on in life. And really, every business seems to be getting bought out at this time. I love small companies and even now support small businesses, but I understand. I really do like the Gart Brothers. They stop in all the time, and we talk, laugh, and dream. As a staff, we decide to keep doing what we are doing, and I don't think most customers realize we have even been bought out. Things are different in the store, but it is not a bother. During the first manager meeting we have, Ken Gart goes around the table and asks each manager their plan for our individual stores—what do we want to be known as? I tell him, "I want us all to live on kibbutz and live and work together." He laughs so hard because he knows I really mean that.

BE. THAT. PERSON.

A while later, Finish Line becomes the partner in the buyout. Finish Line is a big company that sells much more than just running shoes. So now my deficiencies as a manager get much more pronounced. Again, I understand big companies coming in. The problem isn't the buyout; the situation was more me within a big company. I am spending more and more time in a back room on a computer. I am answering emails, doing end-of-day reports, having conference calls, and being involved with inventories. I know you are thinking, "Ummmm, Collette, that is pretty much what a manager does." But for me, it isn't what I want. It is now a job. I love the people part of the job, the run groups, coming up with fun ideas to get people together. I always tell people that as a manager, I am 99 percent people, 1 percent business acumen. I love the company, but I guess I just don't care what our sock to shoe ratio is. I do end up learning so much about profit and loss and a whole bunch of other stuff I can't quite remember. I am realizing that I have taken Littleton as far as I can, and someone with a business mind and who is more into metrics should come in. The company agrees. I really want a community outreach coordinator job, but there is no such job—or is there?

GOODBYE, C. H. O. P.

Everything seems to happen in time lapse speed at this point. They move a new store manager into the store and my house goes on the market. Yes, the Cutest House on the Planet, the house that for four years has been the dream home for Tater and me. The house that every journal entry starts with "I love my house!"—that house is for sale. Greg, again, is phenomenal as my real estate agent. The weekend it goes on the market, I have over fifty showings. Pat and I take turns taking Tater out of the house. At the end of the weekend, I have thirty offers, can you believe it? Thankfully, Greg narrows it down to two. I have a choice of 100% net profit and all cash, or a much lower offer, but they include a nice letter and a cute picture of their basset hound. I actually have a hard time deciding, but, I decide that the first offer, with more money, will pay off all my bills and still give me some money to start my new adventure in Cincinnati, Ohio. Yes, indeed, BRC says that I can go be a community outreach coordinator in their Cincinnati running store. As an added bonus, I will be closer to my immediate family.

Now I come home, and I explain to Tater what is going on. "Tater, we are moving from everything we know and moving from this cute-as-a-button house to go start a new job in Cincinnati, Ohio. You won't need your snow boots, but I hear you will need an umbrella. I guess it rains, *a lot*. We will have a blast, I promise!"

" My answer is yes! Don't forget to pack my marrow bones!"

One person I will be saying goodbye to is this awesome gal named Courtney. When I interviewed her for a job at the store, she said, "I am a spaz, and I forget things all the time."

"When can you start? That is a perfect mix for us!"

She is so incredibly talented at web design and really anything artistic or computer-related. One day, she comes in to work with this cool bag.

"Where did you get that? It is so awesome!"

"I made it," she replies.

"You sew too?"

"Yep!"

"Well, I have these jeans that are my absolute favorite, and I haven't been able to wear them because they have big holes. Do you think you could find some really fun patches and bring the jeans back to life?" I tell her the story of the jeans.

"For sure, bring them in!"

So I do bring them in. And life goes on. She has a baby and I wonder about my jeans, but I am not going to tell her, "Listen, I know you have a six-month-old baby, but do you have time to fix my jeans?" And then I am leaving BRC and as a going-away gift, she hands me the jeans. They now are more awesome than before. The patches are so fun and so cute, and I don't ever want to take these jeans off.

And there it is. I punch out for the last time at BRC on April 21, 2016. I am back to feeling excited, nervous, scared, alone, and expectant. However, this time on my new adventure, I have all these people rooting for me. This time, social media and texts will keep us connected. I feel almost like I am living in another world as I am leaving my friends, my family, and my life. It seems like an epic move, and I am so excited to see what the next journey is, but at the same time, leaving this family is almost more than my heart can take. These are people who, when I was in a dark year of my life, came into my life and became my friends. They rallied around me, helping me to shed thick skin, and they cheered for me all along the way. I will miss them more than words can say. I am excited to see what is next in my journey, and it isn't anything I am expecting.

These are the friends I miss everyday still! Here we are at our annual "Not Your Momma's Turkey Trot!"

CINCINNATI, GET READY

The worldly goods I am deciding to pack into the U-Haul make me laugh to this day. I pack *everything*!

Half box of cornstarch—check

Snowshoes—check

Little yellow vase—check

Old candles—check

My thinking is that if I bring everything, then it will be easier for Tater and me to adjust. The best realtor ever says, "Collette, you know you can buy all this stuff in Cincinnati, right?"

My friend Keith, who helped me move into my house and is now helping Pat move me out of my house, says, "It took a pickup truck and three small cars to move you in. Now look!" But I just keep taking everything, and I still laugh.

I spend the day and night saying goodbye to my Colorado family, these people who I have experienced all events of life with—birthdays, weddings, funerals, bat mitzvas, Christmases, Thanksgivings, vacations, roller derbies, outdoor movies, amusement parks, graduations, graduation parties, high school musicals, pro soccer games, cross-country meets, births, all of it! Pat, Tater and I will take off after I close on my house the next day.

The best realtor ever calls: "Ummmm, Collette, closing on their house got pushed back a week, so we can't close on yours."

My heart sinks for many reasons. I want to be all done, money in the bank, and take off and start our new journey—and also because I am going to go look at a yellow VW van before I head out, which I already know I will love (no one knew this, not even Pat). It has those old-school green checkered chairs, a little fridge, a cookstove, and a little sink. I have to call and cancel the sale as I wouldn't have the money, and they had someone on the waitlist for it if I didn't come up with the money. I can just see myself tooling around my new city with Tater hanging out the window, but it isn't to be. It only dampens my spirits for a little bit because the next day, the three of us leave to drive 1,100 miles to Cincinnati, Ohio—Tater and me in my little red Chevy Sonic and Pat following behind in the U-Haul filled with winter sports equipment I will never use, an electric woodstove that I will use, and enough running clothes to never wear the same thing twice.

Pat and I still talk about how amazing this trip was. It's not like we see any wonders of the world, but all three of us are so caught up in the magic and a road trip to a new city. We camp at a KOA campground our first night. Again, it is nothing spectacular, but everything about it is filled with excitement. Tater even senses something new and thrilling. The next day, we get caught in a deluge of rain and get separated on the road, and even though that is frustrating, again, even the frustration seems new and exciting. We stay in a hotel in Illinois that night. On Mother's Day 2016, we pull into Cincinnati with a U-Haul and a car full of dreams.

Pat and I get everything moved in and out of boxes. I am one of those people who unpack everything that day! The house is beautiful, old, and all redone with huge windows and shiny wood floors. When I flew in to look at the house a month ago, I thought the stairs to the two bedrooms and bathroom would be too steep for Tater, and indeed, they are. I decide to make the first floor our house. I set up a living room and a bedroom and still have enough room to host a square dancing party if I so desire. Pat agrees to stay two weeks to help Tater adjust and to put in another doggie door.

Pat and Tater join me on my drive to my first day of my new job. Whatever direction Google Maps gives me will be the way I take every single day. It's who I am. Tater is in the back seat with her head out the window. Pat is in the front seat with his head inside the car. We are high-fiving and excited. I pull down the driveway and run right over a squirrel and kill it. I go from sparkly to crying in a matter of seconds. Is it a sign?

The first week, I end up working fifty-five hours and realize it is indeed *not* a community outreach coordinator job. I am doing the exact things I was doing in Colorado. I call someone higher up than me and say, "I thought this was supposed to be a community outreach position."

"Regardless, you are there now!"

All my years of working for a company that I loved summed up in "Regardless!"

The second week, Pat leaves and heads back to Colorado, and we have a torrential downpour with high winds, thunder, and lightning. I love this, but Tater isn't the biggest fan, and unfortunately, I am at work. I text my nice new neighbor and ask her to check on Tater.

She calls: "Collette, Tater was sitting in the center of the back porch in the driving rain. She was so sad and drenched. I took her inside and dried her off with these big fluffy towels and put the dog door down so she couldn't get back outside."

I get home that night, and she is still a little wet. I take one of those fluffy towels that my neighbor dropped off and wrap her in it. I sit with her on the couch, holding her and telling her how much I love her.

During the third week at my new job, a gentleman about my age comes into the store. I greet him and ask what brought him in that day. He tells me he needs to get a new pair of running shoes but would not let a woman fit him for shoes. I tell him I would find a male, and I do. I get home that night and pick all fifty pounds of Tater up, carry her up those steep stairs, and put her in a hammock I had hung in one of the bedrooms. I climb in there with her and say, "Tater, I am going to do something so nutso!"

"Oh, I have seen you do some pretty nutty things before," she says.

"True, Tater, true! My heart and soul are getting tested again. This time, instead of just growing thick skin and putting up with pushing those feelings away, I am going to listen to my heart." I tell Tater that she is in her last years. "I am hoping for so many more, but at twelve years old, I promise to make your senior years epic."

We sit there for an hour, me petting her and composing a resignation letter in my head. The next morning, I send the letter and it covers most things a breakup letter mentions:

"It's me, not you."

"Lately, everything has felt wrong."

"This job has lifted me to some great mountains, but it has run its course."

As with relationships, there are offers of different stores or different jobs, but I decide not to move Tater again. Three weeks into an epic journey, three weeks into what I thought would be another dream job, my resignation is accepted. I do what all mature people do when they don't know what to do: I cry and scream "ugh" into my pillow and mostly sit staring at the walls for literally five hours. Tater, bless her heart, goes about the day like she is living her best life ever.

I decide to take a cue from Tater. I can sit here and dwell on all I left in Colorado, or I can make the absolute best out of this situation. Life doesn't always go as planned. The Cutest House on the Planet sold, and I have a little bit of money. So, Tater, let's live life with gusto. Let's make your senior years wild and epic because, really, "Regardless, we are here now."

IT WAS AWESOME!

Sixty-four.

Yes, sixty-four times I will use the words "awesome," "amazing," or "great" in my journal in what turns out to be the two months I will take off to decompress. While I was writing this chapter, my Google search history looked like this:

What is a synonym for "awesome"?

What word can I use instead of "amazing"?

Is there a better word than "great" to use?

Never would I think that selling the Cutest House on the Planet would end up leading to some of my most epic adventures. I tell Tater that I have no place to be today. I have nothing scheduled or planned. She says, "Welcome to my world, Collette." I feel scared, nervous, and scattered but excited. Our days end up looking like a Cincinnati blog.

"Tater, there is a clambake at the park today."

"Grabbing my bib, Collette."

"Tater, a kickball tournament! Let's go watch."

"Putting on my shin guards."

"Tater, donuts as big as my face about an hour away."

"Let me grab the camera."

"Tater, I found a trail with swinging bridges we can run across."

"Lacing up my trail shoes, Collette."

I am absolutely loving it. It is *amazing*.

I am doing things every day that I love. I find all these butcher shops that still wrap your purchases in paper. One of these shops, called Humbert Meats, is right by Tater's vet. They saw marrow bones in half for me, and I buy a bagful. They also have the best ham salad and stuffed pork chops. I go to bookstores, come home, and sit outside and read all afternoon with Tater right next to me. I cook, grill out, or look at recipes and try new things. We sit on the back deck. She chews her marrow bone, and I drink a beer, margarita, or prosecco. We find a new park or a new trail every day. If the paper says it will be too hot for animals to be outside, we sit in the air conditioning.

I try to do something wild every day. One day I wrote in my journal, "I spent $150 at the bookstore." I think that is pretty wild. Our most favorite day, though, is Saturday. We head to Findlay Market. Findlay Market is what I think the world should look like. There is poverty but also people who seem to be fiscally fluent. There is every ethnicity, men dressed as ladies, dogs everywhere, and everyone seems to be getting along just fine. You can see generations of farmers, butchers, merchants, and chefs whose great grandparents had a dream, and that dream is still alive. I love that Tater and I can walk the mile down this big hill. If the paper warns us of heat, we drive the mile down.

For most of my life, I made my friends through work or run groups, but I have neither right now, so I am making friends along our adventures. Some of the first friends I make are the Wildeys from Wildey Flower Farm. I know right away they have big souls. They ooh and ahh over Tater and then hand me a huge bouquet of wildflowers. Tater and I walk uphill all the way home smelling these blooms and coming up with recipes to use all the veggies and meat we just purchased.

AIN'T NOTHING GOING TO SLOW TATER DOWN

One hot day, I leave Tater at home and go on a run. When I get home, she isn't sitting in the air conditioning like I thought she would be. She is outside on the back deck, which seems different. As I get closer, I see that she is blown up and looks like a Macy's parade balloon. I don't have much knowledge of bloat, but I know that is what has happened. Because she is such a long dog, her stomach is suspended like a hammock and can twist. I also know that it is fatal and needs to be taken care of immediately. I am so thankful for my brother's fraternity buddy, Dave, and his wife, Karen, who have been helping me adjust to life in Cincinnati. One of the first things they gave me was the name of a great vet clinic named Grady Vet that they use and is open twenty-four seven. This is still one of the best pieces of information I've ever received. I can call anytime and go there anytime to pick up prescriptions without an appointment.

I head there and call them on the way. It is about a half-hour drive. The vet is hesitant to do the surgery because of Tater's age. I assure her that she is healthy and runs with me every day. I even tell her Tater stays inside when the newspaper tells her it is too hot out. I am scared and am just talking.

She says, "OK, it is pretty invasive. We will attach the stomach so it can't turn again. We will need $3,000 beforehand."

I assure her, "Tater will come out of it just fine, I know it!"

I hand her a credit card and, for the first time in years, I know I have the money on it. I am reminded again that what seemed sad selling that awesome house has turned out for the good. I am a wreck the whole two to three hours of the surgery. The surgeon that day ends up being Tater's regular vet from there on. Her name is Dr. Quilles. I am so incredibly thankful to Dave and Karen for sharing this info. Tater makes it out of this surgery, and the vet still talks about how she didn't think Tater would make it because it was such an invasive surgery and because of her age. But she comes back spunkier than ever, ready to conquer the world.

After a couple weeks of recovery, we are back exploring every inch of Cincinnati either by car or foot. She is feeling so great that we take the four-hour trip to see my family. I love sharing her with them. Sure, she finds a bag of cat food and starts eating it. Sure, I was a helicopter mom, saying, "No, don't go there, come here, Tater" incessantly, but we played Back Alley Bridge and had a blast.

I always call my mom when I am about fifteen minutes away from my house, and I do this time too. I just keep telling her how awesome it was that Tater got to come. I tell her I love her bunches and hang up. Tater and I pull up to a red light, her head is out the back window, and we are both feeling so great. A car pulls next to us, and their hip-hop music is just blasting. Tater starts barking and barking, almost to the music. The guy rolls down his window, laughing, and turns his music up louder with Tater barking to the beat.

We come home, pop open some prosecco, and sit on the back porch, looking at the stars and wondering what the next day will bring. Phew, we are having a ball!

So, what would you do if you had two months to do anything? Me, I spent time with my passions: hanging with Tater, reading, exploring new places, cooking, coming up with recipes, running trails, making new friends, and making the most of a situation I never saw coming.

BE. THAT. PERSON.

It really was awesome, amazing, great, incredible, magnificent, spectacular, phenomenal, out of this world, extraordinary, unbelievable, wonderful, and Google mentions *amazeballs* as well.

THINGS THAT GO BUMP IN THE NIGHT

It's the middle of the night, and I wake up because I hear a sound. I don't quite know what it is. I stand up and don't see Tater in her bed, and I realize what I am hearing is Tater trying to walk up those steep stairs. I also notice that it is thundering and lightning and a pretty cool storm outside. I realize Tater is scared, so I go pick her up and carry her the rest of the way up into this huge walk-in shower. I grab a bunch of blankets to put down and my sleeping bag and a pillow. We sleep in there until morning. It is the most beautiful thing. Tater feels safe and secure now. Every storm, she knows she can somehow get up those stairs and sit in the shower.

But she won't have to do it for long as Kyle, who runs the management company I rent from, comes over and says, "Collette, you have been here for almost a year. Instead of renewing here in this big house, let's go check out this place two streets over. It's on a little cul-de-sac. It is a bottom unit in a multi-family home. See what you think."

We go over, and I almost cry. It is absolutely perfect. It has a huge cast-iron bathtub, gas stove, wood floors, and sooooo much natural light, and he will allow me to put in doggie doors again. It is seven hundred square feet of pure joy! Every day, I walk Tater over so she can get used to this new place. Pat comes at the end of May, and we move everything over by my car or by walking it over. We even carried over that awesome blue couch I bought when I first moved to Littleton. People in the neighborhood stop us for months, talking about how we carried Tater's doghouse: "Hey, weren't you the ones with a bean bag chair on top of your car?" It ends up being such a wonderful place. I wouldn't even have known there is a couple that lives upstairs because they are so quiet. And each couple after them is great as well. It is a perfect place for Tater and me to live out her senior years.

BACK TO WORK

"Well, Tater, we just can't keep going to get donuts as big as our face. They cost money. I need to find a job. Now what should I do?

Tater says, "Why not ask Google?"

"Great idea! Google, what should I do next in my life?" Darn if Craig's List Cincinnati doesn't come up. I find a job opening working for the city of Cincinnati doing all their flowers around the city. I fill out the application, get a response, and set up a time to meet. I mention in the interview that I was a flower girl in Steamboat Springs, Colorado, twenty-two years ago. I am sure that is the reason I got the job.

It is such a cool job. I get to ride my bike every day to work and back. I also realize that indeed it does rain a lot here, and we work in the rain. I drive around in a big pickup truck with a water tank on the back. I get to plant and then take care of all the flowers downtown, so I see such cool neighborhoods and I get to know my way around all the streets. I have had a handful of managers in my life who were appreciative and approachable and made me want to do a great job. My manager at this flower job, Ann, is one of them. Everyone, it seemed, had a degree in horticulture, trees, or some type of green plant science. I drove a golf cart around twenty-five years ago, watering planter boxes and flower gardens. But Ann never makes me feel "less than."

BE. THAT. PERSON.

Many of the people I work with are quiet and reserved. I am wide awake at 6:00 a.m., ready to play carpool karaoke in our work trucks. Again, Ann accepts that part of me and always gives a hearty good morning to me. Because the job is seasonal, I will be done working soon and it is no surprise then that when the job does come to an end two months later, she has a going-away lunch back at the shop for me. An outsider would have thought I worked there thirty-five years. She has huge donuts shaped like cakes and all my favorite candy spread all over the table. Had she handed me a gold watch, I wouldn't have been shocked. I hope some time in your life, you have a manager like Ann who was accepting and patient. She really threw her awesome confetti my way.

Since the flower job is seasonal, I decide to get back into waitressing. It will give me a little more bang for my buck if you will. One day while I am watering flowers, I see a sign outside a restaurant called Taste of Belgium that says they are hiring. They have a couple of bistros spread out over Cincinnati. They are opening a new one right on the banks of the Ohio River between the pro football and pro baseball stadium. I walk right in—baseball cap, reflective safety vest, legs dirty from dragging water hoses—and the man who comes over doesn't blink an eye. He has me fill out an application right there.

I interview a couple of days later with a gal named Erin and tell her that how I am there in the interview is exactly how I am in real life, even at 6:00 a.m., and if I would be a good fit, great.

She responds, "Yes, it would be hard to pretend to be as gregarious as you are."

I end up starting two weeks later. It takes me a little bit to get back into waitressing, but I do like the job, and it seems to be a good fit. One day, I come back to the server station and say, "I don't think my table likes me."

"No, they don't like you. You are their server."

"Shoot, because I really like them."

"Collette, you need to get thick skin if you are going to stay being a server."

"Hahahaha, no way. It took me seven years to peel my thick skin. I am not growing it back ever again."

AND MAINE MAKES FIFTY

2017—Scrolling through Facebook one day, I see that my friend Angie posted one of those "Of the fifty states, check the ones you have been to" memes. I realize I have been to forty-nine states. The only one missing is Maine. My mom tells me that when I was five or six, we went as a family, but since I don't remember it, I didn't count it. I call Pat and tell him to block off all of September as Tater and I are headed camping in Maine for three weeks and he must go too!

If I were to make a list of memorable places I have been to, it would include the following: I have seen the northern lights and Mount McKinley in Alaska. I have watched Old Faithful erupt and splash in Yellowstone. I have attended a private wedding on a beach in Maui. I have seen Mount Rushmore and climbed my fair share of fourteen thousand foot mountains in Colorado. I have seen the moon set and the sun rise on the same day on an island in Georgia. This trip to Maine makes that list as well.

I have noticed a bump starting to form on Tater's face about this same time, and her vet tells me that we will just see what happens.

Traveling at the speed of Tater is the theme of this trip, and she definitely is the MVD, (Most Valuable Dog) not only in traveling, but also in Acadia National Park. Our campsite sits right outside the park in Bar Harbor, and we can watch the sunset over the water right from our tent. Our days are filled with long runs or hikes, and at night we eat lobster and drink beer around a campfire. One day, we pull up to the entrance to the park, and the ranger at the kiosk says, "I need to see your park pass, please." Before I can reach into the glove compartment to get it, Tater sticks her whole head and torso out the window. "Oh, hi, Tater. We know you! Head on in and have fun. Bye, Tater."

Another day, we are at the top of Cadillac Mountain, and it is raining sideways. The wind makes Tater's ears stand straight out. I can barely see anything, but I still want a picture at the top. Just then, from some random car that is driving by, I hear, "Tater, Tater, Tater. Hi, Tater!" I don't recognize the car.

A week later, a woman comes running up to us as we are walking to our car.

"Hi," she says. She is almost out of breath. "We just lost our two bassets within the year. Would you mind if I sat and just pet your dog?"

"She would love that."

The woman sits there petting Tater and crying. A year after Tater died, I would do the same thing to a friend I had met through Instagram. I sat and petted her basset hound, Betty, for an hour.

Everywhere we go, Tater makes friends and makes people smile. That's just who she is.

We enjoy three weeks of trail runs, tent camping, eating amazing lobster, and seeing incredible views of Penobscot Bay from tops of mountains.

By the numbers:

- Two—numbers of showers I take in a ten-day span.

- Two—car cell phone chargers I go through

- Seven—days in a row I eat lobster

- Eight—hours it pours one night

- Eighteen—number of donut holes Tater eats

- One—number of apple cider margaritas I drink

- Three thousand—miles driven to make some epic memories

- Too many to count—comments like these: "Can I pet your dog?" "Can I take a picture with Tater?" "We had a basset hound growing up"

- Fifty—states I have been to

Tater and me enjoying the view after a great run up the mountain in Maine.

A NEW TASTE OF BELGIUM LOCATION

I come back from Maine changed and feeling like my soul is overflowing with confetti. I keep wondering how the heck I can make money camping around the US with Tater. I go to Taste of Belgium and also wonder if waitressing really is what I want to be doing. I call a friend of mine, Michael, who was a manager at this Banks location but transferred to another TOB location. I tell him I'm not sure serving is for me. I am going to start looking for some other job—but not sure what—and ask if I can use him as a reference.

"Collette, you are coming to this location [Rookwood]. You will love it."

"I don't want thick skin though."

"My friend, I have no idea what you are talking about. Just transfer here with me. I promise you will love it!"

So...I transfer, and guess what? I love it.

My first shift was January 1st. I still laugh about everything that went on during that shift. Servers were crying. It was so flipping busy, and I was so glad to have a three-table section. How would I carry those heavy trays all day? The whole brunch shift flew by, and I felt at home. Everyone seemed to accept me. I walked out the door with $250 in tips and couldn't wait to tell

Tater all about my new work family. I would end up working at this location for two years.

This family of ours spends days talking about our dreams and passions, but these people don't just talk about them—they make their dreams come true. One person is now a model, some are in school, some are nurses, some are becoming nurses, one plays in a band, another helps with a high school marching band, and one has an online art studio (now a brick and mortar studio—she was the one who tufted the smiley face patch you see on the back pocket of my most favorite jeans). Throw in people who love computer games, sing in the opera, a ballet dancer, and, yes, a guy who wants to start a fish taco truck. Indeed, we made one heck of patchwork team. They see me through so many fun and busy and nutso brunch shifts, and they also see me through my darkest day.

BEACH BABES

The bump on Tater's face seems to be getting bigger, and her awesome vet says, "Collette, we can't do radiation on her face, and we can't remove it because of where it is. You just keep giving her the best amazing life, OK? Also, if her nose starts bleeding, bring her in immediately."

So, I call Pat. " Block out April. Tater has never been to the beach, and she is demanding to go before her beauty bump gets too big." Because Pat still has Colorado as his home base, he either drives or flies into Cincinnati. This time he flies, and he will be flying with Frontier Airlines. I love that they have some huge, cute painted animal on the tail of their planes and always look forward to what animal he gets. He texts as he boards: "It's a fox!"

As Tater and I drive to the airport to pick him up, his plane flies right above us—so close we can almost touch it. We see the fox and start yelling, "Yay, yay, yay!" We love the first night that Pat gets into town. It's paella night! Pat and I put on our aprons, make paella, drink rioja wine, and dance around to the Harry Connick Jr. station on Pandora. Making paella takes time, and the smells just permeate the house. Lemon zest and saffron and chorizo all mix. When we finally sit down to eat, all we say over and over is, "Mmmmmm," "Mmmmmmm," "This is amazing!" and "Oh my!" Yep, every first night he gets into town is the same, and I love it! It is one of my favorite traditions we have.

We are leaving in two days, and we still don't know what beach we are going to. We have decided to spend five days in Asheville, North Carolina, as I have never been and I want to run trails on the Blue Ridge Parkway, go to breweries, see the Asheville Tourists stadium (at that time they were a minor league baseball team for the Colorado Rockies), and go to Vertical Runner Running Store in Black Mountain (now Mountain Running). We stay at a KOA campground outside of downtown Asheville, and the fun starts. One morning, Pat sneaks out and gets donuts and coffee. It was so fun sitting there in the dark in my sleeping bag sharing donuts with Tater. Also, that morning, I am on my phone and see that Pat's cousin is at a beach on the coast of Georgia, and it looks stunning. "Well, let's go see this amazing Jekyll Island, Pat. What do you say?"

"Hip, hip, hooray!" was Tater's response.

We decide not to camp when we get to the Jekyll as we found this cute carriage house not far from the island for a great price. I know I have said it before, but this trip was epic. We leave Asheville and the mountains and start heading to Jekyll Island. You can see the topography changing mile by mile. We suddenly are in green, lush palm trees. This carriage house is simply the best.

We get up the next morning to find the beach. I buy Tater this huge colorful beach umbrella that she can sit under and contemplate life. She digs holes in the sand and just lies in them. She's covered in sand, and I proclaim her first day at the beach a triumph. We find a place selling fresh peel-and-eat shrimp right off the boat, take a bucket of them back, and devour them.

Every morning, we wake up and head to watch the sunrise on the beach. Then I pick up food to make a picnic with, and I always get some of this jalapeño pineapple beer I am in love with. My journal everyday said, "And Tater did great!"

I go on runs, and Pat and Tater go look at historic things. Jekyll Island is absolutely amazing. It is not built up and has no big box stores or fast-food restaurants. When we need a break from the sun, we find some local restaurant. Our favorite is The Wharf—oysters, seafood gumbo, mahi, and mango daiquiris.

We go to the neighboring island of Saint Simons. They have more shops, grocery stores, and restaurants. Both islands are very dog friendly. After a week, we move to another VRBO house two blocks from the beach. It has a fenced backyard, which Tater loves, and it also has a bathtub that I love. A typical day is filled with sunrises, beaches, sitting, reading, napping, or just watching the water. I run into the water when I need to.

One day, we find a secluded beach, and there out in the water are dolphins swimming by. Another morning, we get up before it is light out to go watch the full moon set over the marsh side of the island, and then we drive to the beach and watch the sun rise. Simply amazing! We take off the next day, but our adventures are not over. We head north toward Savannah and end up at this KOA in Yemassee, South Carolina. We stay in one of their little cabins, and I can't believe this is a campground! They have a full coffee bar, beer on tap, and wine tasting every night. We spend a couple of days at Hunter's Beach and Beaufort S.C. My journal says this: "How can I sum up what this whole month has meant to me? I honestly can't. It was that great and once again, Tater was" MVD" And I come back changed again, and again wondering how I can buy a yellow VW van and camp around, love people, and get paid?

Tater loved the beach as long as she had her umbrella!

WHAT BUMP?

People are starting to notice Tater's big ol' beauty bump on her face. Some people ask about it, but most see it and look away. Some will pet her everywhere but on that bump. I remind her daily that only the most special dogs get beauty bumps. One day, we head to go wish my friend Emily a happy birthday. She is the one at work whose other job is working with a local high school marching band. We have a couple fun presents for her, but we are the ones who leave with the best gift. During the break, the students come running over to meet Tater. It is like no one even notices her bump. They get right down to her level and sit there petting her all over, even on that bump. Tater feels so special. I sit there trying to talk to Emily, but I have tears in my eyes with how beautiful these young people are with Tater. The whistle blows, and they have to get back to their tubas and flutes and drums. As Tater and I walk away, we both hold our heads a little higher and our souls seem radiant. Yes, even high school students can have big souls. Everyone needs a smile. Some people need a little more love. Some people just need to know they matter in this world, bumps and all. Smile, tell them, hug them, pet them even! Be. That. Person.

BYE, PAT

September 14, 2018—Tater and I drive Pat the slow, no highway way to the airport. When we get home, I look at my journal of everything the three of us did the two weeks he was here, and it reads like a Chamber of Commerce Facebook post on what to do in Cincinnati. I list ten parks and trails, eight different restaurants or breweries, six farms, ten different meals we cooked together using local provisions, and two trips to the vet. Tater now goes almost every week to get her beauty bump checked, blood work done, and continual help with her autoimmune skin stuff. Her blood work comes back fine. Yay! And now Tater and I start counting down the days until Pat comes back and we can have a paella night. Ten weeks away. He will get here the Tuesday after Thanksgiving.

You see, we have such an amazing time when Pat is here. It is so free and natural. We can both be ourselves. He helps so much around the house and with Tater. He is encouraging, life-giving, calm, and spontaneous. He is also a great driver. Tater can hang her head out the back window, and I sit day-dreaming in the passenger seat. Pat is so good for my soul. I will never forget the night of a huge storm and all the power went out. We three sat eating on the floor by candlelight. It was magical.

Tater and I fill our days with very slow walks, hanging out, doing jigsaw puzzles, and pretty much being best friends. I put the phone up to her ear every time Pat calls so she can hear his voice.

NOW CONSIDERED THE
WORST DAY OF MY LIFE!

October 16, 2018—"Tater, come on. We have to drop these flowers off from our garden to my friend Amy at work."

It is such a beautiful fall day, and we drive by one of her favorite little walks and decide to stop to see if she is up to doing this walk today. It is a short jaunt around this block in this quiet tree-lined neighborhood. All the houses are decorated for Halloween. I think they must be doing a contest. Tater loves this little walk because right toward the end, the house on the corner has set up a small area just for dogs. There is a bowl of water, a bench, and a metal jug full of fun treats. She has a spring in her step today, and as we turn the corner to head to the treats, a woman about my age is coming the opposite way around the corner. She stops to pet Tater. She squats down, looks Tater right in the eyes, and kisses that big beauty bump. She stands up and almost seems angelic. Very calmly, she says, "She has come to terms with this bump. It is us humans who haven't." She walks away. I don't say anything because what can you say to such a statement? Off Tater and I go to get some treats, but her words are still circling in my mind.

When we get to Taste of Belgium, friends come out to ooh and aah over Tater, and some even take a few pictures. We run some more errands and spend the rest of the day at home, me working a jigsaw puzzle, Tater chewing her marrow bone and napping. I grill out a burger, and we sit out back together. It really is such a perfect day. Around 8:00 p.m., we head to bed.

Somewhere around 10:00 p.m. or so, I hear Tater go outside. When I turn over again, I can't remember if I hear her come back in. I get up and check her favorite bed in the living room. She isn't there. I go and look out the window in the kitchen to see if she is out back, and I don't see her there either. I put shoes on and step outside. She is sitting at the bottom of the stairs; I assume wondering what has taken me so long. She once again looks so bloated, but this seems somehow worse, like she is so inflated, so swollen, like she is going to just pop out of her skin. This isn't bloat, this is something that makes my heart race and my eyes cry. I pick her up because she can't move and, for some strange reason, put her collar and leash on—the things we do when we don't know what to do. I put her in the back seat of my car and call the vet clinic. They assure me they will be there to help me get her inside. Once again, I am thanking Dave and Karen for telling me about this amazing clinic that is open twenty-four seven. I keep telling Tater that she is such a good girl. I go the speed limit, if not a little slower. I want to be cautious and also wonder if I just want a little extra time with her. I call Pat and let him know I will keep him updated.

She keeps her head between the seats right by my arm. I start to smell something but can't quite figure out what it is. It's familiar, but I can't figure it out. Have you ever done that with a smell? The smell gets stronger and stronger, but I still can't place it. When I finally get to the clinic, I open the back door to get her out, and the whole back seat is covered in blood. It looks like a murder scene. That was the smell. Blood is everywhere, and she is bleeding out of her nostrils and mouth. Her paws are covered in blood. I carry her inside, and indeed the crew is waiting there to help me. They take her in the back and put me in a quiet room. I remember sitting there and just staring and listening to my heartbeat. Because it is so late, my regular vet isn't here, but the most compassionate, soft-hearted vet comes in to finally talk to me. She says the tumor on her face finally bled out to all her internal organs and she can't live much longer. Again, I am just speaking and not thinking, "Could you call Dr. Quilles and see what she thinks?"

"I have worked with her for seven years, and she trusts my judgment."

"But her blood work came back fine," I say. I ask if she could explain everything to my best friend Pat.

"Of course!"

I call Pat, and she explains that Tater has lost so much blood and is bleeding out internally. Then I hear the most compassionate vet say, "Yes, that is what Collette also said."

He had also told her, "But her bloodwork came back fine." I keep Pat on speaker phone, and I ask this nice vet what she suggests, even though I know the answer. "Can you bring Tater in here in this nice room and send her to the bridge here?"

"Yes, of course!"

When she brings Tater in, I know it is time. I keep Pat on speaker phone as I sing all our favorite songs to her. I end with the Mary Tyler Moore theme song:

"Who can turn the world on with her smile?

Who can take a nothing day and suddenly make it all seem worthwhile?

Well, it's you, girl, and you should know it.

With each glance and every little movement, you show it.

Love is all around, no need to waste it.

You can have the town, why don't you take it?

You're gonna make it after all."

I have my nose on her nose. We are eye to eye, and my hands are on her face—yes, on that beautiful beauty bump—and I repeat over and over, "You are the best! I love you so much! You are the best! I love you so much!"

The vet has a stethoscope on Tater's heart and inserts a tube into her IV. She nods to me when Tater's heart stops. I cry out so loudly it doesn't even sound like me. I am gasping for air because I am sobbing so hard, trying to catch my breath but bawling my eyes out. It is so hard to breathe. Crying, gasping, trying to swallow. The vet doesn't think any of this is weird or abnormal. She tells me to sit in here as long as I want, even if it takes all day. It is about midnight. She leaves and there I sit. My soul splinters.

When I call my mom, she knows right away as it is midnight. She answers and just says, "Nooooo."

I say, "Yes, it just happened."

I call Michael to tell him I won't be at work tomorrow and the rest of the week doesn't look good either.

Pat and I sit there for two hours on the phone. Talking, crying, laughing sometimes, but mostly I am just trying to hold it all together. I send him pictures of Tater just lying there. I don't feel like myself, like I want the world to stop spinning, but it doesn't. I finally get up and find that compassionate vet. I don't remember the drive home.

DIFFERENT NOSTRILS

Tater and I have had many area rugs over our life together. I tell Tater one day, "Tater, we are going to get a fun shag rug so when we sit on it in the winter, it will be warm and cozy." The rug arrives and Tater loves it. No, she *loved* it. She sleeps on it, chews her bone on it, and, for some reason, loves rubbing her itchy autoimmune skin all over it. I bet it feels so great.

One night, we are sitting on the rug together, and I say, "Tater, this rug is really starting to smell like you."

"Yes, I have been working on that smell."

"Maybe I need to get a new rug now, one with different fibers so it doesn't smell so." Yes, I use the words "different fibers" as if I was a rug aficionado. I order the rug, and not soon after, Tater has that appointment with the Rainbow Bridge. I drive home that night from the vet clinic so early in the morning and walk into an empty, quiet house. I lie on that shag rug and cry and cry. Now I think, *This rug smells fantastic.* This rug smells so much like Tater, and it is the balm for my soul. I am smelling that rug through different nostrils now.

The new rug comes a couple days later, and it sits wrapped in plastic for over a year. How often I think of this in my daily life, how I think something is smelly or unpleasant, but, really, if I could change my perspective, maybe the situation is actually warm and cozy. Tater is even teaching me from the Rainbow Bridge to smell life through different nostrils. Yep, I really do want to live like Tater.

LIFE WITHOUT TATER

October 17, 2018—I now start to live my life without Tater, without my soul mate, and I am not sure how to even do that. I feel so empty. Will I ever live with gusto again? She was my everything. How can I bear this grief? It isn't that I don't want to leave the house—it's that the house is different. And instead of wanting to disengage with people, I want to tell everyone about Tater. My journal for months will go into detail just listing all the places I have cried that day. At Target one time, I have to drop all my items and rush to the door because my tears are so overwhelming. One day I head to Home Depot to pay my bill, and I can't even get my debit card out of my wallet. The last time we were there, Tater pooped right there at the customer service desk. I picked it up with a poop bag, and we just carried on.

So here it is the day after Tater died. I have to go see how to get all this blood out of the back seat. I stop by at one of those fancy car washes. An older gentleman comes over, and I open the back door. He gasps. I explain it was my dog, show him fifty-seven pictures of Tater, and assure him it isn't from a dead body. He tells me that they can't touch blood, and then he gives me the biggest hug and says he lost his dog six months ago. These people just keep giving me bits of their big souls, and now more than ever, I am aware of it.

I go to all our favorite stores to let them all know Tater died. I stop in at Grady Vet to see Dr. Quilles, but she isn't in, and I stand in the middle of the lobby just crying. No one even thinks it is weird. But the one thing I really want to do is go to that tree-lined neighborhood. I try looking for that angelic woman. I had never seen her before and have never seen her since. But I go to that house on the corner and knock on the door. A woman answers with a cute dog barking next to her.

"Are you the person who keeps that dog area out front?"

"Yes, that's me."

"You have to know that it makes a difference in this world. Thank you so much for making my basset hound's senior years awesome. Keep doing it." I hand her a handwritten thank-you note from Tater and me.

Cooking is hard. Eating is hard, and for some reason I don't like when the sun goes down and starts to get dark. I keep on these little fun lights, just like I did as Tater got older and needed them on at night.

The people who rally around me are too numerous to count. I am absolutely floored at how many people were touched by Tater and knew what she meant to me. The number of cards, gifts, drawings, and donations to basset under her name are astounding to me. Anna and Greg send me a gift card to Whole Foods as they knew I would forget to eat.

I knew Tater was in her winter years of life, and I just always thought that she would die when Pat was here. The vet would come over to my cute place, and Tater would be lying in her bed, and we would hold her and sing to her as she went to the bridge. Then I would take off to some deserted island for a year with my grief. But that isn't what happened. Pat is in Steamboat Springs painting a friend's condo and has to finish the project, and I can't afford to take off for a year, so here I sit. I sleep very intermittently, and as I drive around Cincinnati; I bawl my eyes out. Every inch of this city is Tater and me. I have memories everywhere. I leave my wallet in so many stores that I go to during these next days.

I need to head back to work; that is the first big step. A coworker asks if they should work for me and I can take some more time off, but I decline as this needs to happen. So much of our life together was about me leaving for work and coming home. That morning, I leave treats hidden around the house just like I always did, and pulling away from the house, I can't even see because my tears are just rolling down my face. I carry my phone on me all day and tell every table I wait on all about Tater and show them pictures. I tell them I want her wonderful life to inspire me to live like she did. I get home that first day, lie on her bed, and fall asleep.

TATER'S ASHES

Pat flies in a week later, and we head right to the vet clinic to pick up Tater's ashes. We take her to all her favorite donut shops and trails and especially to Burwinkel Farms. That was our special place. Do I need to mention that I cry at every place? We take her box of ashes everywhere we go. I place them in the backseat of my car just like she is still there. I pull up to the bank teller, and I ask, "Can I get a treat for my dog?" There are more than thirty treats in the back seat with her. After a week, Pat has to head back to Colorado, and I drop him at the airport four hours early as I told him I need to be home before the sun sets. Darkness, for some reason, scares me lately.

MY FAMILY

Here is my journal entry one month after Tater's death:

"I am feeling a little something worse than sadness. I can't quite put my finger on it. I miss Tater, but it has moved into the deepest part of my soul. It is a grief I have never felt, and it hurts. I continue to be amazed at the outpouring of love from people. It is helping me more than I can describe. I head up to see my family and I can't wait to hug them."

You see, my immediate family has always been there for me. In 2009, not one of them judged me or dismissed me from the family. They stood by me. We don't have it dialed in as a family, but we have love, and that gets me through life a whole lot easier. We yell, laugh, and cry together, and it is good for my soul.

The most amazing family!

MY SOUL IS STILL FRACTURED

And so it goes...Every event, every holiday, every day, I put one foot in front of the other and try and remember to breathe. I do jigsaw puzzles by the dozens, and it helps. I have yet to go running. Running is Tater and me, and it will be months before I can do it. I put my running clothes on and end up on that beautiful smelly shag rug and cry. Missing Tater is present in my soul, present in my heart, and present in my life.

Pat and I celebrate my birthday with gusto, and he surprises me with a Le Creuset Dutch oven. I have wanted one forever. It works perfectly to make paella rice. We donate Tater's food and beds to the local animal shelter. (Yes, four beds. She needed holiday beds, after all.) Not her main one, however. It sits in the living room like always. I still can't wash the bath rug or move her food bowls. It has been almost three years, and I still have her medication chart hanging.

My soul is still fractured, *but...*

This is what it comes down to. Had I known that October 16, 2018, would have been her last day on this earth, I wouldn't have done anything differently. We had the most beautiful day, and I made sure her last years were absolutely epic. I know when she looked me in the eye that night, she said, "Wow, now that was a great life. Thanks, Collette!"

TATER TUESDAYS AND
A NEW ROAD TRIP

Spunky, spirited, and stout!

My journal says that is how I wanted to start 2019, but I am not feeling it. I find it hard to make decisions and don't know whether to stay here in Cincinnati or head back to Colorado. I am not my best right now. I find myself lost and my thoughts jumbled. I am not myself at work, and I seem to miss Tater most on days off.

I am realizing that life without Tater isn't getting any easier, but it is getting softer, if that makes sense. I also feel a pull to do something different than serving. It's not that my shoulder is in constant pain; it just doesn't seem to be making my soul smile. I am starting to look at every table as money, and I don't like that. To help me through all this grief, I start a "Tater Tuesday" on social media, life lessons from a sassy old basset. It really has helped. Tater had it dialed in. I am wading through life and wondering who I am or even who do I want to be? Ha—spunky, spirited, and stout!

While there are still a whole lot of "firsts" to get through without Tater, there is one big one.

I call Pat. "Take April off! I need to do a road trip with you and Tater's ashes. Am thinking just a week of tent camping on the beach. I want to see how I do without Tater on a trip. We have always wanted to go to the Outer Banks. What do you think?"

He replies, "Get the paella ingredients ready!"

The week is absolutely just what my soul needs. Awesome, amazing, restful, and beautiful. We stay at a KOA campground in Rodanthe on Hatteras Island. Our tent site is literally one hundred yards to the beach. Looking the other way, it is another one hundred yards to the sound. Tater's bed is the first thing we put in the tent, with her ashes right in the center.

Every morning, we walk to watch the sun rise on the Atlantic Ocean, and every night we watch it set on Pamlico Sound. We sit on the beach all day, eat lunch at our campsite, go back to the beach, and always end the afternoon at the pool. I ride the fun slide or do cannonballs, and we would end in the hot tub. We meet so many people who help patch my soul back together. They have their dogs with them, and I sit and pet them and whisper in their ears all about Tater. Pat and I fill the week with so many tears, but a whole lot of laughs too. The jack-in-the-box that is my soul is slowly winding up again.

Pat and me at the Outer Banks

HOW HAS IT BEEN A YEAR?

October 16, 2019—I can't believe it has been a year. I can't believe I just went through every holiday, every event, and every day without Tater.

One year later and here is what I look like:

- I still cry over missing her

- I still talk about her every day

- I no longer ask the bank teller for treats

- I can walk into a dark house but still sleep with her fun lights on

- I haven't washed my bath rug yet

- My soul is still fractured, but it seems confetti and smiley face stickers are doing a good job of patching it up

- She remains my example of living life to the fullest

Year two almost seems to be starting out harder as I no longer have the "firsts" to get through.

FINDLAY MARKET, HERE I COME!

November 2019—"Pat, I don't know what I am going to do next, but I am ready for something different. I know what I don't want to do. I don't want to manage again. That just took it out of me."

Two weeks later: "Pat, you won't believe it! JT, the manager over all the Taste of Belgium bistros stopped by the restaurant and one thing led to another and I am going to be the manager at the Taste of Belgium at Findlay Market!"

"Of course, of course, you are!"

My friend JT has a gold medal in hugs! You meet him, and you just want to hug him even if you aren't a hugger. He had stopped into the Rookwood Taste of Belgium, where I have been working the last two years, after a hearty hug, we start talking and he just randomly says they are looking for a manager at the Taste of Belgium at Findlay Market. My eyes get big, and I say, "Me, me, me! I don't have a résumé, but I need to apply." And just like that, JT is my new boss! I can't believe I will be working at Findlay Market. My heart feels so big!

I walk down every day or ride my bike if I need to carry anything home. If it is dark, I just wear a headlamp to guide my walk. It is simply magical. Why I seem to start new jobs at the busiest times is still a mystery to me, and this is no different. I start the week before Christmas. I call JT every fifteen minutes crying and telling him I need to quit.

He keeps saying, "You got this, Collette. Just get through Christmas."

I keep calling, and now my calls go right to voice mail. But indeed, with his help and the help of another manager, David, I do make it through, and I do learn how to do food orders and commissary orders. I still don't understand the schedule app, but I handwrite the schedule, and it works. I can't believe I get to work at Findlay Market.

Sunday, March 15, 2020

I leave work early to go pick up paella ingredients! I will pick Pat up in a couple hours. He will stay for about a month, and we are planning one quick camping trip so that I can run up Mount Mitchell, the highest mountain east of the Mississippi. The paella night is awesome—dancing, cooking, drinking, and saying "Mmmmm" over and over again. We get up Monday morning, and the world looks a little different. We pack a picnic and head on a run, but the restrooms are closed at the trailhead. That night, I get a call from my huggable boss, JT, telling me that all the Taste of Belgium restaurants are closing for dine-in service, but Findlay Market location will be staying open as we are an essential business. Tuesday, JT calls me at work to say everyone is laid off and it is just me for the rest of the day. Only twenty employees remain for all of Taste of Belgium bistros. COVID-19 has now changed the world. That night I am asked if I want to stay on with a pay cut. I really didn't even think about the answer; of course, I will stay on. They tell me I am allowed to choose one person to work with me. I choose Ashley for many reasons. She is a single mom of four kids and lives right there by the market, but most importantly, she will stay positive. I know it.

Ashley and I start down this COVID path as best we can. We feel so disposable every day. People hand us credit cards and cash straight from their bras to pay for things. We try and sanitize and stay safe, but every little cough is suspect. People can't even touch our waffle packs, and we have to get their coffee and cream as everything is now behind the register. Wearing a mask in front of a five-hundred-degree oven is unbearable, and people stop in to tell us they are making an extra $600 a week on unemployment. If we let it get to us, it could, but we won't let it! Ashley and I are making the best of it and actually having fun. Pat walks me down every day and comes early to pick me up to help with dishes at the end of the day. Ashley now calls him "Mr. Closing Dishes." Pat and I walk home and pick up fun beer curbside from Rhinegeist Brewery and cook some great meals from provisions from the market.

We are spent emotionally and physically at the end of the day, but we continue to stay positive and just keep showing up. Hugging people isn't allowed anymore, and it is killing me. Ashely and I figure if our oven mitts can withstand five hundred degrees, if we put them on, they should keep us safe for some COVID hugs. We now call them our huggin' gloves! Ashely is simply amazing. Her soul is big, and the confetti she throws around sticks to me like glue. I love her! She really is *that person!*

BE. THAT. PERSON.

Ashley and me with the huggin' gloves on!

Pat ends up staying seventy-three days. We never get the chance to camp and run up Mount Mitchell, but he must finally head back to Colorado as people are now starting to travel again and they need him to dog sit. We decide the theme for his COVID time here was "We did so much when we couldn't do anything."

MY BEAUTIFUL SISTER MARILYN

I am in my mom's big, huge boat of a car with my sister Marilyn driving. She is the only one who can handle this tank. We are going over to my brother's house to play Back Alley Bridge. We don't turn on the normal road, and I ask, "Hey isn't that the turn?"

"No, we never go that way," says Marilyn. Something seems off. On the way home, we pull into one of those drive-through liquor stores that seem to be everywhere in Ohio so Marilyn can buy cigarettes. The man working says, "I always have to ask for an ID, but just tell me your birthdate." Marilyn is looking in her purse for her driver's license.

I say, "Marilyn, just tell him your birthdate." I realize she doesn't know her birthdate.

A month later, I am back up seeing my family. I walk into my mom's house, and Marilyn says, "Cricket. Cricket."

"Oh no," I say, "Where?"

"Cricket."

My mom comes out and says that Marilyn needs to go get her phone looked at. She uses Cricket.

"Ohhhh!" Something seems off. We talk a little on the way there, but I realize she can only answer yes/no questions. When we get to the store, a man with a gentle, kind spirit helps us. She just needs to pay her bill it seems, so he shows her where to put her debit card and then where to sign. She just looks at the screen and looks at me and then looks at him. I realize she doesn't know how to sign her name. I sign for her, and he lets me. I wish I would have asked his name because he was so patient with her.

During another trip up to see my family, Marilyn really can't play our Back Alley Bridge anymore as she can't tell suits apart.

By the end of the year, she will be in a memory care home in the dementia wing that has twenty-four seven help available. COVID hits again, and we can't go see her. It is more than my heart can take. She loved all people and all animals. Growing up, we had every stray animal that she would bring home. She was a free spirit and a hippie. And now she doesn't know how to talk on the phone and says "holy crap" incessantly. We finally can see her and hug her, and I know her soul is still in there.

The best siblings in the whole world! Marilyn is in the dress. Ohio!

BONDED PAIR?

July 2020—*Pop!* Yep, I open a bottle of prosecco. I'm not celebrating anything. I just love prosecco is all. I sit on the couch after a long day at work
and get on Instagram to say hi to all my friends. An amazing basset rescue I
follow, Basset Hound Rescue of Southern California, has a post saying something great about a basset that just went to their furever home. The post ended
with, "Link in bio if you want to apply for a basset." Is it the prosecco or Tater
whispering in my ear? I apply and get a phone interview.

During the interview, the nice woman tells me not to get too excited as
the waitlist may be a year long. It is almost a relief to hear that as I am still
unsure if my soul is ready. I get an email back saying that I was accepted and
have been put on their waitlist. I simply write back and thank them so much
for accepting my application and can't wait to see who will waddle into my
life. I can do young, old, or even a bonded pair. Yes, I use "bonded pair" in a
sentence. I don't even know what that meant, really. A couple days later, an
absolutely amazing woman named Felicia, writes back, "*What?* You will take
a bonded pair? We have a pair coming, and no one else said they would
take a bonded pair."

I tell her I am open to the idea, but only if they don't die. She says she can't
guarantee that. And so, it starts...I am nervous, excited, worried, stressed, and

oh my gosh, I can't believe it. I call Pat and tell him. "Would you like to see pictures of them and see what you think I should do?"

"Nope, I already know the answer."

I call my sister Tootie to tell her. You see, during the last couple years, she and I have really been getting close. Oh, we loved each other before, but now, I feel she is one of my best friends. She has been through things and has a big soul because of it. I tell her how nervous I am about getting two dogs, and she assures me that it will be tough, but Tater is happy.

THE JOLLY TRIO

August 19, 2020—Pat and I get into Oklahoma and find a camping spot. It is dark out, and we are putting the tent up. We open a beer, and I can't really speak. I am not sure what I am feeling. Tomorrow morning, we will pick up Jolly and Buster and my life with those two will start. I hope it is an epic, adventure-filled life, full of love and huge smiles. Let this be the next step toward everything that lives in my heart and soul right now. I sit there crying, holding my beer and Tater's ashes.

August 20, 2020

Jolly and Buster run out the front door and right into my life.

The Jolly Trio! Me, Jolly, Buster

Donna, the foster mom, hands them off to me, and I tell Pat, "Let's take them camping!"

Off we go. They do so great on their first camping trip, and we start making our way back to Cincinnati. I had been reading about bonded pairs and really start to understand the connection they have. It is a healthy relationship, not an aggressive one. They share everything and feel safe with each other. Buster loves watching over Jolly. They share their food, water, and treats and are a great team even though they have different personalities.

I read up on how to train them to introduce to them to their new home. I asked the rescue and the foster mom if Buster and Jolly know how to use a doggie door, but neither knew if they could. We pull into my place, and I take them on a leash to the little fenced backyard and tell them this is their new home. I take off their leashes, and they both run straight to the doggie door and inside—my question was answered. I run to the front door, and we all pig pile on my bed. Buster gets up, goes in, and pees on the bathroom rug, the only thing that I still hadn't washed from Tater. He never marks a single thing again. I know Tater told him to do that to get me moving!

I take them down to meet my Findlay Market family, and Ashley says, "You're going to leave here, aren't you?" She could see it in my eyes. I was smitten!

It has been almost two years since I had a dog in my life and even longer since I had a young dog in my life. I realize these two are spunky, spirited, and stout. I tell them all about Tater, and they keep saying, "We know, we know. She sent us to you!"

I take them running on trails all over Cincinnati and Kentucky, but I start realizing that Buster would rather lollygag, sniff, and occasionally sprint for one hundred yards. I say, "Yep, I don't need to make you a runner. You be you, Buster." When Pat is here, he hikes with Buster behind Jolly and me as we run for miles.

And, yes, September 19, 2020, is my last day as manager of Taste of Belgium Findlay Market. I love the job, the market, and especially the staff, but I realize in 2021, I will be sixty years old. I want to see what is next with my life and I desire to be with these two as much as possible. We are becoming a bonded trio!

January 1, 2021

Jolly and Buster and I are in a flow.

They seem to be flourishing, and their personalities are shining. I think Buster is almost human, and I actually wouldn't be surprised if one day he walks into a party, starts introducing himself around and telling funny stories, and then leaves. Someone then asks, "What was that?"

"Oh, that is just Buster! Isn't he awesome?" He is large and in charge and full of delight. He lets Jolly and I know when it is time to wake up, when it is time to eat, when it is time to go on a walk, and when it's time to stop and smell the flowers on our walk. He makes me laugh.

Jolly is soft, demure, gentle, and smart. She crosses the street to say hi to any young child, and it is so lovely. She has perfected stop, drop, and roll and drops at every person we see so they can pet her belly. She is a people pleaser and is so obedient until there is a squirrel running by.

We have adventures during the day that involve us seeing and experiencing every inch of Cincinnati, and at night we flop down on my bed, Buster all the way under the covers and Jolly with her head on my pillow beside me. We thank Tater again for bringing us together and for making us spunky, spirited, and stout!

I did find two part-time jobs, one delivering eggs and produce for ETC Produce based at Findlay Market, and I also help an old server friend from Taste of Belgium, Jeremy, who did get that fish taco truck up and going. It is called J's Fish Tacos! Both jobs allow me to spend more time with Jolly and Buster, but also just as important, I get this crazy idea to look back on thirty-five years of journaling, and I decide to write a book about my life and adventures. You see, on December 14, 2021, I will be sixty years old, so I wanted to look back and see—have I lived a life I dreamed of? Have I made a difference in this big world? I'm wondering if my life was as full as I thought it was. Have I lived with zest and gusto? I know some people think that life is short, but I don't. I sometimes thought life was very long, but I do think life is fast. Had you told me while I was drinking 3.2 beer out of plastic buckets after rugby games in college that someday I would be sixty years old, I would have laughed and been confused.

What I thought I would find in my journals are pages of epic adventures, off-the-wall shenanigans, and unbelievable road trips, and I did indeed find that. *However*, what I was amazed to find was that my life has been filled with these extraordinary people. Some were people I knew and some I only met briefly, but all these unique individuals are what has made my life dynamic, people from all over the world who have thrown their soul confetti into my life, and I am forever changed. Campground rangers, managers, Amtrak workers, friends, family, Instagram dog lovers, random people along the road, and trail running buddies, all making a difference in this world and in my life. And it gets me excited, then, to wake up each day and hope to pass on some confetti or hugs to others. Some days are easier than others to do just that. But not every day, as some days I am the one needing the smile or hug. I now realize life is like that, the "yays" with the "ughs." The "woohoos" with the "Did I really say that?" Yep, life is journey, a rollercoaster made up of all different seasons, and not one will last forever.

I have had a top-of-the-line washer and dryer in my house. I have had to wear my bathing suit bikini bottoms for underwear because I couldn't afford to do laundry.

I have sold my house for 100 percent profit. I have declared bankruptcy.

I have had over one hundred pairs of new shoes in my closet at one time. Today, I am wearing a pair of shoes that have holes in them that I use for mowing the lawn, running, and working on the taco truck.

I have made $337 monthly car payments. I have gone three years with no car.

I have given money to homeless people. A homeless man gave me money as we were at the local food bank once.

This is life! And life is meant to be shared!

I now realize that I can be warmhearted with a broken heart.

I can be jubilant but cry.

I can be gregarious with a soul that is fractured.

I don't have an IRA, but I have journals filled with experiences, adventures, and people. Yes, page after page of people who gave pieces of their soul to me so that I could flourish and become fully Collette!

I do believe I can radiate love, acceptance, compassion, zest, and a desire to be that person no matter where I live or travel to, because it isn't where I live, but how much confetti I throw along the way.

JUST SOME RANDOM JOURNAL ENTRIES!

I found so many entries along this journey that made me laugh, smile, and cry, but I just couldn't make chapters out of them:

- The world was supposed to end today, but I am glad it didn't as I got a $434 bonus from work.

- Don't let me interrupt people while they are trying to tell a story.

- I went to dollar oyster night. I got six oysters and a $33 lobster roll.

- Great things are waiting for me if I dare to go after them.

- Every time I see a camping picture, it makes my heart excited.

- No one at my new job thinks I am funny.

- Got my nose pierced today for my fifty-fifth birthday.

- My first check was for $650; I must find a second job.

- My bank doesn't have check registers. When they finally get some for me, the dates on the back calendar are from five years ago.

- I seem to be a little emotionally stable today.

- I lost forty pounds and never found it again.

- We got rid of our television and fifteen years later, I still don't miss it.

- Since Bucket died, I have no one to talk to about work.

- I seem to use my downtime to grow and dream.

- First Christmas in thirty years outside of Colorado.

- My soul feels incredibly sad today. I hope it is just menopause.

- I want to bring a smile to someone today.

- I want to be alive expecting miracles.

- Magnanimous—something that is alive, big soul.

- I don't always pay attention when people talk to me.

- Let me root for people, cheering them along through life.

- Things I love: parades, sunflowers, donuts, thunderstorms, smiley face anything, jigsaw puzzles, cranberry sauce, baths, sunrises, foot-long hot dogs, new, clean sheets on my bed, tan lines, puppy bellies, ice cream trucks, fireplaces, Christmas music, when kids' softball or baseball teams go out for ice cream after their games, Honeycrisp-apple-scented anything, and the smell of campfires.

- Things that I don't really like that much: sticking my hand down the garbage disposal, dirty microwaves (especially in a work setting), having to change passwords, hoodies, flat tires, ceiling fans or box fans, dressers, and hiccups.

Oh, one last picture!

My friend Andy! He would have made a great maid of honor!

Big hugs! Go be that person!

9 781685 150464